Manager and Team Develop......

Manager and Team Development

Ideas and principles underlying Coverdale training

Bernard Babington Smith and Alan Sharp

BUTTERWORTH
HEINEMANN

Butterworth-Heinemann Ltd
Linacre House, Jordan Hill, Oxford OX2 8DP

 PART OF REED INTERNATIONAL BOOKS

OXFORD   LONDON   BOSTON
MUNICH   NEW DELHI   SINGAPORE   SYDNEY
TOKYO   TORONTO   WELLINGTON

First published 1990
First published as a paperback edition 1991

British Library Cataloguing in Publication Data
Babington Smith, Bernard
   Manager and team development: ideas and principles
   underlying Coverdale training.
   1. Management. Theories
   I. Title   II. Sharp, Alan
   658.4

ISBN 0 7506 0316 X

Printed and bound in Great Britain by
Redwood Press Limited, Melksham, Wiltshire

Contents

Foreword by John Adair   vii
Preface by Bernard Babington Smith   ix
Introduction by Alan Sharp   1
1 The warrant for management training   6
2 Early courses and early lessons   8
3 The development of a systematic approach   13
4 Open and closed situations   18
5 Decision theory and the turbine theory of action   21
6 Problem solving and a systematic approach   24
7 Learning styles and a systematic approach   26
8 Action learning and a systematic approach   30
9 Observation   32
10 Improving observation   36
11 Purpose and choice   42
12 Specifying aims   48
13 Task and process – and the balance   51
14 Assessing performance and talents   54
15 The doctrine of success   57
16 Steering and joining   60
17 Leaders and followers   67
18 Delegation   71
19 Getting to yes – and getting to know   74
20 Proceedings and transactions   79
21 Individual and team development   92
22 Development of teams   97
23 Systems and systems thinking   103
24 Organizations and organizing   112
25 Organizations and a systematic approach   116
26 Organization development   118
27 Boards of directors   124
28 Systematic approach – possible developments   130
Appendix 1   135
Appendix 2 Open and closed systems   146
Appendix 3 Terminology   150
Bibliography   157
Name Index   159
Subject Index   161

Foreword

by

JOHN ADAIR

Coventry Cathedral one sunlit morning some twenty-five years ago was the setting of my first meeting with Bernard Babington Smith. By chance we both had friends on the staff of the Cathedral. We instantly recognized our common interest and have remained in touch ever since.

The themes of our many conversations and letters are most ably set out in this timely and welcome book put together by Alan Sharp. Initially Bernard explored the differences between the Coverdale approach and my own. For both our approaches had drawn upon a common source in the 'group dynamics' movement in the United States during the late 1950s, but they had developed in distinctive ways. But our conversation soon transcended this issue. Therefore I was able to explore some of Bernard's thoughts that had either not been taken up by Ralph Coverdale, or, if they had been adopted, had undergone considerable alteration subsequently.

Clearly Ralph Coverdale and the Coverdale Organisation have been the chief beneficiaries of Bernard's sustained thought; others – such as myself – have drawn directly or indirectly upon his wisdom. His distinction between purpose, aims and objectives is just one example of a seminal idea which has become an integral part of my own teaching.

What I think is so useful about Bernard's thinking is that it focuses upon the essentials or basics of our chosen field. In that sense he is as much a philosopher as a psychologist. Simplicity and elegance are the hallmarks of his ideas. They are not couched in unattractive jargon. He exemplifies Einstein's dictum that 'everything should be made as simple as possible, but not more simple'. Perhaps that is not surprising, for his mind was formed in a tradition in which philosophy and psychology together held each other's hand in the moral sciences.

Knowing my own debt, for some years I have been pressing Bernard to write a major book. I have even threatened to publish it myself! Bernard's natural medium, however, has been the letter or paper addressed to friends in his own handwriting. But such is the volume of his correspondence over the years to members of the Coverdale Organisation and to other friends, that even the task of editing a selection of them would have proved to be a daunting one. Still, all is not lost, for those archives will one day prove to be a rich mine for doctoral students intent upon research.

Alan Sharp, who shares both my admiration for Bernard and my keen sense that his contribution to our field merits its full recognition, has now stepped into the breach with this very good and comprehensive exposition of Bernard's main themes of thought. A valuable refresher course for some of us, but for many more it will be an introduction to one of the leading British thinkers in this field. It will also help to ensure Bernard's place in the history of our continuing exploration of 'the human side of enterprise'. Here, then, is a fitting tribute to a great teacher.

Preface

by

BERNARD BABINGTON SMITH

Thirty years ago in 1959 Ralph Coverdale invited me to help him in developing a new system of management training, in which managers would learn 'to take responsibility for managing men'. A similar invitation nowadays would talk of managing people!

In the earliest courses my contribution was mainly to their structure, but soon I became an active member of a small group of people that ran them. As the Coverdale Organisation grew in size my participation in the work changed from direct involvement in running the courses to helping to train, guide and advise those who ran them. This included planning and conducting seminars for groups of Coverdale staff as well as discussions and exchanges of correspondence with individual consultants.

With the passage of time I have come to participate less in the active work of the Coverdale Organisation, perhaps this has allowed me more time to think – hence the original proposed title of this book – 'Thoughts on Getting Things Done'. Involvement in the work has throughout been most interesting and I am grateful for the opportunity to take part in such stimulating work.

In thinking back to the early courses, it is interesting to recall the enthusiasm that accompanied this work. This was very noticeable among those running the courses, but there was also evidence among participants. It is important to recognize now that such enthusiasm is often to be found and is of itself no guarantee of the value of the work being done. It is clear in retrospect that enthusiasm needs to be backed by reasoned argument and findings that can be used in everyday dealings.

This book is a collection of comments on aspects of Coverdale training, designed to contribute to its power and effectiveness. While the comments are all based on letters and papers that I have written, I am clear that I would never have brought myself to undertake the labour of putting the various components together. I am deeply indebted to Alan Sharp and thank him most sincerely for his contributions to the book by correspondence, conversation and, by no means least, by the labour of producing the text.

Introduction

by

ALAN SHARP

A major aim of this book is to record the significant and influential contribution to the field of management training made by Bernard Babington Smith. The greater part of that contribution has been made over a period of more than thirty years through the incorporation of his ideas into the body of methods now known as Coverdale Training. He was the co-originator of that training with Ralph Coverdale and many of the original and important ideas which were significant in the success of the whole approach stemmed from him; both before and after the death of Ralph Coverdale he provided guidance to members of The Coverdale Organisation in the continuing development of ideas as the field of work extended. 'Coverdale Training' would not exist today had it not been for Ralph Coverdale's energy and enthusiasm and the ability he possessed in such great measure to fasten onto valuable ideas and put these across to others. For that reason it is right that he is remembered in the name which the training bears and for that reason Sir John Harvey-Jones (in *Making It Happen – Reflections on Leadership*) describes the Coverdale System as 'a British invention developed by a management genius called Ralph Coverdale'. However, it is without question that Coverdale Training would be quite different, and arguably much less successful and valuable as an approach, but for Bernard Babington Smith's contribution. That contribution, as this book attempts to demonstrate, was made both in the form of important ideas of lasting value which he originated and through the efforts he made to ensure that errors and disadvantages did not creep in as developments took place.

The book is not intended to be a history of the development of Coverdale Training, although, because B.B.S. (as he prefers to be referred to) contributed so much to the early development of that body of methods, much of the content is inevitably closely linked to Coverdale Training. Even less is it intended to be an appraisal of that training or a description of what is covered in full by the term 'Coverdale Training' at the time of writing. While links with the roots remain clear, the field of work of the Coverdale Organisation has widened greatly, particularly in-house training and consultancy. Anyone seeking a complete description should contact the organisation.

A second aim is to try to make available to a much wider audience the many significant and valuable ideas which B.B.S. has developed himself, or helped others to develop, in the fields of management and organization development.

B.B.S. has published very little himself. Indeed his response to my attempt some years ago to persuade him to do so was that he had spent his life trying to reduce things to essentials and it appeared to him that writing a book meant that you would have to pad them out! It is true that many of the ideas have been and can be contacted by those attending Coverdale courses. However, while this number is significant, it is still only a small proportion of those to whom the ideas are likely to be of interest and potential use. In addition, despite B.B.S.'s close association with the Coverdale Organisation as consultant and adviser, it would be surprising if even those ideas which have become key elements in the body of methods generally recognized as Coverdale Training could be appreciated in full as a result of attending one or two training courses run by consultants without his experience of seeing how those ideas developed. In fact a description of the way in which the ideas developed over several years, how they arose, how and why they have been modified, has undoubtedly helped my understanding of them and will, I believe, assist that of others, no matter how great or small their existing acquaintance with the concepts.

What the book tries to show, through a series of short essays, is how a number of important ideas and concepts related to getting things done have developed. The sources have been discussions and correspondence between B.B.S. and myself, letters written by him to others, his notes for talks and papers given at various times, mainly to Coverdale Organisation staff, and one or two pieces of previously published material. As far as practical I have used his own words, and in many cases have quoted verbatim from his written material.

In a paper entitled 'On technical aspects of Coverdale Training' read to the IUC/EAMTC International Workshop Seminar at Trinity College, Dublin in September 1967 B.B.S. said 'I believe that underlying this work there are principles of the utmost importance, and I see great advantages arising from it, trying the while never to remain blind to disadvantages or errors that may creep in.' Also he has remarked in conversation that he felt often in his work with Ralph Coverdale (and no doubt with many others of us whom he advised in our Coverdale Training activities) he found himself waiting for an opportunity to correct some error or other, and if he waited long enough he generally managed to do so. This book contains one or two examples of such corrections.

Why should 'disadvantages and errors' creep in to any system of training? As B.B.S. suggests, the most significant reasons relate to the distinction between, on the one hand, what can really be regarded as general truths or principles that will always hold and what, on the other, should more sensibly be seen as ways of looking at things or teaching devices. The value of the latter lies in their use at a certain point in someone's development, and within certain contexts, in assisting that person to make sense of what is happening. Where such 'teaching devices' are treated as general truths then errors creep in. (See for example Chapter 15 – The doctrine of success.)

It should be stressed that many such 'teaching devices' have proved of great value in helping individuals to take a fresh look and subsequently modify the way they do things and deal with others. Nevertheless, it remains important that those introduced to them, whether through training courses or through reading books, should be encouraged to see them and treat them as 'teaching devices' and not as 'general truths'.

A similar point has been made by B. A. Farrell in his commentary on a number of small group methods in *Training in Small Groups* (edited by B. Babington Smith and B. A. Farrell). He points out that the practitioners of different methods develop what he describes as 'Ways of Talking' (or WOT for short). These enable those using them to understand and describe what is happening in those terms. However, there is in his view no evidence to suggest that such WOTs are 'truths' providing a provable explanation of what is happening and it is misleading of practitioners to imply this.

Another potential cause of errors creeping in may be found in the way in which systems of training develop. It is clear that as practitioners try out ideas, observe and review what happens, they wish, in order to assist later delegates to learn, to convey what they themselves have discovered. Thus training which starts in the spirit of joint discovery (for both staff and students) develops to the point where students are in practice being encouraged to learn what the staff have previously discovered. As time passes and the staff change, the new staff may be conveying what they themselves have learnt from their predecessors. It is not difficult to see how, through such a process, differences of real understanding arise between those (like B.B.S.) who made the original discoveries and those who have been introduced to the ideas subsequently. In this way developments can lose touch with the original roots and misinterpretations, errors and disadvantages arise.

By sketching out how many of the ideas contributed by B.B.S. developed both originally and subsequently I hope this book does something to lessen the risk of such errors.

The ideas themselves may be seen as related to three themes:

1 The development of groups as observed through studying their proceedings on Coverdale courses over a period of some thirty years.
2 The development of individuals through examining what experience in such groups seems to mean to an individual and how it can help.
3 The consideration of situations involving transactions between people as individuals and as members of different groups (as opposed to their proceedings when members of the same group).

While there is not a completely logical progression of topics through the book, some attempt has been made as far as seemed practicable to arrange the sections and not leave them as a series of unrelated essays. Thus the book starts with the early development of some important ideas and with some general points about Coverdale groups (by which is meant groups which have some common aim and where the individuals have made the choice to help each other in some sense). Succeeding chapters look at what this means to an individual and how it can help him or her. From this the book returns to the group and how a group's proceedings work and thence to transactions where the question of individuals' loyalties is involved in ways far beyond those relevant in considering the internal proceedings of a group. Finally it moves on to ideas relating to organizations.

While his experience of laboratory work in psychology and his wartime experience in the Central Interpretation Unit of the RAF were important influences, the effective starting point for the development of the ideas covered in this book was in 1959 when Ralph Coverdale approached B.B.S. and asked whether he would help him develop a new approach to management training. At that point two streams of thought and experience joined. Ralph Coverdale with experience of businessmen, with A. C. Nielsen's and the Steel Company of Wales, had recent experience of T-groups and held strong views about Freudian-based interpretations he had met in this connection. He had been impressed by the effects on individuals of being in a group and also of the risks of approaching what happened in terms of some theory or other. In particular he had been put off by the theory sessions he had met on a course when the staff expounded accounts of what was going on, in terms of depth psychology or of a Freudian approach. B.B.S., with the experiences noted above, held strong views about the need for exploration and discovery as a method of learning rather than instruction or the usual confirmatory forms of laboratory work; and about the progressive and coherent development of investigation and ideas from the familiar to the unfamiliar. He also held strong views about Freudian Theory. It is typical of B.B.S.'s approach to any question that his initial reaction was to wonder why it should be necessary to train managers at all. The reasons he found, which are set out Chapter 1, still remain extremely convincing arguments – perhaps the most convincing that can be put forward. Numerous reports have been published over the years attempting to make out a case for much more training of managers. In my own view B.B.S.'s arguments seem much more likely to influence those many very senior managers who, not without justification, remain sceptical about the value of almost any form of training for managers.

1

The warrant for management training

Very early in his association with Ralph Coverdale, B.B.S. raised the question 'Why do managers need training courses?' As he pointed out, 'Surely business has been conducted by human beings for thousands of years and into the history of business are woven the histories of thousands of people who have begun at the bottom and worked their way up. In the process thousands have become effective managers.' Such sentiments have often been expressed subsequently, particularly by very senior and successful managers themselves, in pointing out that their own success has been achieved through experience, without ever attending a training course in management. No matter how many official reports over the years have argued a case for much more of such training in the UK in particular, the top managements of very many companies remain unconvinced. It seems therefore an appropriate starting point for this book.

In considering this question it is helpful to look first at the principles of training in general and then see whether these principles are applicable in the field of management and, if so, how best they may be applied. It seems clear that there is a need for training when someone's equipment in skills, rather than in ability, is not adequate for the tasks to be undertaken. The situation of need arises from a discontinuity in the task, either because a person is called on to face a task at a different level (usually higher) of difficulty or because some innovation leads to the need for a new skill.

The particular discontinuity we are concerned with is that in some sense there is a sudden change in a person's relationships with fellow employees when he or she undertakes a managerial assignment. Another aspect is that where people take tasks for which they are fitted, they may be expected to improve with practice, but that where their jobs change, or are to change, suddenly, training is owed to them. Thus one form of 'managerial training' can be seen as that taken when someone reaches and crosses into managerial territory.

Continuing with the theme of training in general, there are two obvious stages and a third not so obvious which is, however, of very great importance because if it is included we have a system which is in a sense self-regulating and self-perpetuating, thus giving a powerful form of continuity to an organization which adopts it.

The first thing to ensure in any system of training is that good habits are adopted by the trainee. What such habits are depends on the nature of the enterprise, but it is self-evident that an organization of any size will benefit if its employees are taught/learn to do things in certain ways. A good example of such training is to be found in that provided in the armed forces. Second, once employees have developed habits it is important that they should take a fresh look at these habits, and, by seeing them in the setting of experience, learn what is useful about them, and what may be discarded or developed. The learning in the second stage is different from being taught in the first, since it carries within it the development of some understanding of the principles involved. When similar thinking is applied to the particular case of management this gives the first two stages of management training needed in any organization of size. The first is that as a matter of routine the newcomer to management should be taught the practices of management adopted by the firm; the second that when a manager has developed these practices to the point where they become habitual, he or she should go on a course designed to make managers think about these practices and their justification and to think for themselves how to act in the face of unfamiliar situations.

The third stage, which if included makes an organization into a system which is in a sense self-regulating and self-perpetuating, is that periodic conferences should be called for senior management at which the current plans for training junior management are made known, enabling top management to appreciate and comment on these in the light of their own greater experience.

2

Early courses and early lessons

The first courses for managers which were developed by Ralph Coverdale and B.B.S. had three components:

1 'Course project' meetings
2 Demonstrations
3 Lectures

'Course project'

The group sessions were almost unstructured, with groups of eight to ten meeting, with a consultant and observer (both staff members) in attendance. Each group was told to 'form a group'. The main point in adopting such an open approach was that 'you learn best and remember best what you discover for yourself'.

Much of the work of these groups, despite the fact that the T-group type situation drew the bulk of the interest of the participants, was immensely frustrating, although often an impasse was broken by some sudden insight or 'discovery'. Some important lessons emerging for the staff were:

1 That 'doing something together' was beneficial and contributed to the 'formation of a group' or in other words tended to lead to a group 'jelling'. Action was seen as clearly contrasting with talk or discussion, producing a different psychological climate and bringing a release of tension. B.B.S. noted a particularly striking example with one group that had been becoming progressively more dull and bored. He says 'At a certain juncture I went along a passage beside a courtyard in which cars were parked. What I saw was a group of men cleaning cars with expressions on their

faces which I described to myself at the time as looking as if they had just announced their engagements. The depression in this group had been dispelled by going into action.'

2 A complementary finding was that to get a group together and give it inadequate or obscure instructions was a good recipe for producing frustration.

3 While action was seen as of very great importance, it was also observed that groups were slow to discover for themselves that progress could be made by doing things as opposed to just discussing them.

4 That even when groups did realize the importance of action, they evinced great difficulty in finding things to do.

One situation that arose in the second course had a lasting effect on the design of later courses. In B.B.S.'s words 'It was suggested that the two groups should be redivided into three and that these three groups should be given the same general task with variations, thus: the general task was to draw up a list of the principles of good management; but each subgroup had a subsidiary instruction. One group was asked to draw up such a list for an organization in which the overriding principle was maximum profit, for a second it was maximum improvement in interstaff relations and for the third maximum efficiency.'

'What was striking about the exercise was not the merit of the reports produced, but the enthusiasm with which the groups set about the task. I think this was what started the method of providing things to do as a means of developing teamwork.'

The above experience and findings pointed to the view that in the time available (the earliest courses were two weeks, but soon what became the basic course was one week in length) it would be preferable to structure situations in some way. Thus it became usual for staff to suggest or provide 'something to do', which in time came to be referred to as 'the task'. Originating in this way, the task was 'something to do' offered to or provided for a group as an aid to their own efforts to 'form a group' or 'jell'. It was not a task laid on or something which the group was ordered or instructed to do. This aspect of the nature of a 'task' in Coverdale courses has been a source of misunderstanding and is a feature which distinguishes 'course situations' from, for example, those obtaining in business.

Demonstrations

In the earliest courses, demonstrations were of two kinds – aspects of visual perception and aspects of 'problem solving'. The outstanding lessons of the perceptual demonstrations were that there are great differences between individuals as to what they report having seen in a few seconds, and that therefore most eyewitness reports are more or less unreliable. The other set, dealing with reasoning and the solving of problems, helped to bring out and emphasize the distinction between open and closed situations, a distinction which has remained important ever since.

Lectures

These were given at pre-arranged points in the programme in the earliest courses and concerned topics which were judged to be of general relevance, such as accident proneness and theories of personality. It soon became clear that this arrangement led to difficulties, because what was offered might not be appropriate to the stage reached by the groups. It became progressively less usual to include set lectures; but course directors or others might use general sessions for appropriate input.

Since in review it became very clear that the course project was the feature that had caught the interest of participants, and to a far greater extent than either the demonstrations or lectures, the design of the course became centred on the work and development of the groups. Since too it was deemed preferable in the time available to tackle emotions and feelings appropriate to structured situations (rather than those aroused in the structureless situation of the initial courses), the group work came to be centred around the carrying out of a succession of 'tasks' provided by the staff. This helped to emphasize the value of action in a world of talk, not only because it produced a different psychological climate and brought a release of tension but because action is essential for getting things done, the function of business men and managers.

Following the first two courses, at the Steel Company of Wales, Ralph Coverdale moved to the Esso Petroleum Company, where more courses were planned and run building on the earlier experiences. To B.B.S. two particular incidents were memorable for the further development of the method of running the courses.

1 'There were in the group two or three salesmen. When people were describing meetings in their departments, one of these salesmen explained that, when they had quarterly meetings, about a quarter of the time was devoted to discussing what had happened; the rest was devoted to planning. This led to talk of "planning" among others in the group. One member denied that he ever planned. Someone asked how he spent his weekends. It emerged that he had a yacht somewhere, and that at weekends he would go to it and it might be that he would paint or repair it. This clicked for me with another story I had encountered at Oxford when a Newfoundlander, a clinical psychologist, had said he used to meet people from outlying bays and that the way they thought was so odd. When asked to explain, he said they make no plans; if the weather is suitable they go fishing, or if not they do something else. From these anecdotes emerged a principle that there can be two ways of planning, either to work out in advance what you propose to do, or to have yourself and your equipment in such a condition that whatever turns up you can act appropriately.

2 'The second incident arose when Ralph and I, on the basis of observations, proposed to two sub-groups that they "examine the proposition that knowledge of results helps learning". It was a dull February day. One group of five ensconced themselves in the lounge and discussed the question. The other group took golf clubs and balls out to the little course there was at Esso House. Then they set themselves, taking turns, to chip balls over a fold in the ground onto a blind green. The question was, whether knowledge of where the ball went helped the player to improve his performance. The results of this exercise were quite interesting. Some of the players had played golf, others, I think, had not. It became clear that, when a player had already some skill, he knew himself whether he had played a good shot; so the information "four feet beyond" or "two feet short" helped him very little. He did not need it. If the player had no previous experience, he was not able to make use of this information. This pointed very clearly to a principle, that if someone is making trials, the information which will help will need to be adapted to his level of skill. This group returned to tea well pleased with themselves. The other group in the lounge had driven themselves into the ground arguing about the meaning of the question (e.g. whether there could be learning without knowledge of

results), and were thoroughly disgruntled. About now it was found that if, in making the programme for a course, demonstrations were designated at certain stages, there was no guarantee that the demonstrations chosen would be relevant to the stage of development of the group. This led to a proposal that a stock of demonstrations should be available to be used as appropriate. This was later overriden by the view that not only should there be a stock of demonstrations available, but the staff on courses should be capable of producing demonstrations to suit the needs of the moment.'

3

The development of a systematic approach

The inductive method and exploratory approach of the training continued to be developed throughout the early courses. Ralph Coverdale had brought to the work a deep mistrust of lecturing and the whole system of conveying information to people, often quoting the adage that you cannot *teach* people, but may help them to *learn* for themselves. In recalling what he had himself brought into the training in this respect, B.B.S. noted, 'I had developed an exploratory approach based on the view that, in psychological work, it is not practicable to follow a strict experimental method in which all variables but one are controlled, and the effects of varying that one are studied. For years I had found one could not foresee the variety of factors which emerged in the reports of subjects who took part, in spite of attempts to produce completely controlled situations. This had led me to develop an exploratory approach where only a few factors or conditions were controlled and other relevant matters were explored through the responses made by different people. Using an inductive method, reports on situations or events made by different observers were compared and collated, and generalizations were made as information accumulated. Such generalizations will not be general laws, but statements based on the experience of people concerned; they may form a basis for action; they may become accepted as rules of thumb (and if found to hold generally may come to be treated as principles on which to base behaviour).'

As the courses continued, with the design centred on the work and development of the groups and using this exploratory approach, many discoveries were made by participants. However, the staff learnt from those participants that they could not explain on their return to work to the people they worked with, what it was they had learnt. In addition, many people went away from courses with enthusiasm but then found it difficult to apply what they had learnt. In some the enthusiasm survived, but in others it wilted and died away. This led to two principles:

1 Enthusiasm is not enough.
2 Experience, realization or discovery of something is not enough. It may be of value as knowledge, but for it to be of use one must be able to apply the new knowledge; something which requires practice. Learning to learn is not enough.

In addition, the conclusion was reached that the staff could not know what particular difficulties a person would encounter on return to work, and that therefore they should try to equip people with a general method for tackling difficulties or a framework which would be applicable anywhere. This conclusion led to the gradual development of such a method which came later to be called a *systematic approach to getting things done*.

At a very early stage in their work together B.B.S. had propounded to Ralph Coverdale the view that the difference between open and closed problems would be important. He had done some thinking on this issue and had written a paper in the mid 1950s. The interest had begun years before when, 'I came across an American view that, in the modern world, one did not need to be able to work out solutions, what one needed was to know where to go, what books to consult i.e. to find solutions.

'I linked this view with the effect of true–false tests and multiple choice tests on education; that, when one relies on such tests, pupils growing up believe that questions like those in tests are to be answered in terms of what you have been taught! I felt this approach would be disastrous, for in the long run no one would be able to think for themselves. I suggested that it was most important to distinguish between closed problems such as one finds in arithmetic books where there are lists of answers at the end and open ones where there aren't.' Put another way, he pointed out that in practice much of education did deal with 'closed problems where the answer was to be deduced from the data, and how the preponderance of this kind of work tends to close people's minds and leads them to act on the assumption that a "problem" has a solution. I felt that in the real world one does not know whether the situations in which one finds oneself have solutions, but it is often clear that something has to be done. Ralph Coverdale jumped at this saying that managers often faced situations which were open, but where it was of the utmost importance that something should be done.' The distinction between open and closed was therefore brought into the work at an early stage.

From early courses were learnt the importance of common comprehension among people, particularly of aims, of gathering relevant information, of planning and of action, which was seen as essential. It was then held that out of the task, the aims and the relevant information, one needed to extract or distil the problem. 'Setting the problem' was seen as a particular and valuable skill and it was seen to be desirable to have a 'problem setter' in any group. Shortly afterwards B.B.S. suggested that the phrase 'what has to be done' be used instead, partly because this helped to avoid the term 'problem' (with its overtones of a solution to be found).

Another point that came to prominence in the early 1960s was the distinction between analysis and synthesis, with, as B.B.S. describes it, Ralph Coverdale viewing the former with growing mistrust, and expressing the view that to talk of 'learning by experience' was misleading, that experience alone does not produce learning. From this came the emphasis on review of action and the importance of including the fruits of observation for study and on incorporating the fruits of review in any further work.

Thus by this time a number of stages were seen as desirable in connection with any activity – information as to the state of the case, someone to 'set the problem' or state what had to be done, planning, action and review, and then a fresh cycle.

Ralph Coverdale was talking of thought and action, 'thought a framework for action'. Also about this time, murmurs were heard that the way of approaching problems had already been worked out by scientists and that what he should adopt was scientific method. B.B.S held that whatever one did there was a strong case for being 'systematic' about it.

Various terms were introduced for the procedure which was being evolved. These included 'systematic learning' and 'systematic thinking'. However, a manager at the Whitegate Refinery of the Irish Refining Company, Seamus Roche, suggested that a more active-sounding name should be found. As he pointed out, 'This name leads some students into thinking that they are being introduced to a system of pure reasoning, and they feel they should be working out syllogisms rather than going into action.' He also expressed the view that it ought to be clear that it led somewhere.

Shortly after this B.B.S. proposed that what people in business were there for was 'to get things done' and that the whole procedure was properly to be seen as a 'systematic approach to getting things done'. To his mind it was 'an approach' because it comprised an orderly succession towards action, and also an approach in the sense that, if the first action was not successful, one could try again, and if necessary again and again.

What was never pointed out, in B.B.S.'s recollection, was that while in the world of courses to think in terms of such repeated attempts was quite reasonable, in the real world it could well be that if a first attempt was not successful a second chance might not arise. Here one can see a deep-seated contrast between 'a systematic approach to getting things done' appropriate to a world where 'something must be done' and one may try and try again building each time on past experience and a world of 'finite problems' which require 'solutions' and may never recur.

The method was thus seen as a general method, a programme for tackling any situation, needed because one could not foresee what situations people would find themselves in after a course was over. It was designed to ensure proper preparation in terms of agreed aims. It ensured action and it was a programme for learning from experience, because it included review of performance and so allowed for later attempts to be tackled more effectively. It was devised for, and seen as, particularly appropriate for managers in business (primarily middle managers), since it did not presuppose that there was a 'problem' for which the correct solution was to be found; and it was coupled with the view that the job of a manager was 'to get things done'.

As originally promulgated in 1965, the approach was seen as a complete 'system', envisaging successive cycles of preparation, action and review, in relation to a purpose, continually incorporating fresh information supplied by observation, thus ensuring progress. The system has been called applied logic; so in a sense it is. Anyone who has learnt logic will recognize the rightness of the succession of steps. The difference lies in this, that logic is concerned with the coherence of statements and of itself never gets anything done, whereas this approach is concerned explicitly with achievement.

As B.B.S. later pointed out what was found in working with groups and was built on, was that, 'though one can regard and decry ''a systematic approach'' as nothing new, the ways in which different people actually set about a task are extremely various. There is an enormous advantage in having an agreed system which a group can use without bumping one another's corners. For instance, some people, when they talk of an aim or an objective, think in terms of something two or three years ahead, while others habitually look only a week or two forward. When such a difference can be brought into the open common comprehension can be achieved. Similarly two individuals can mean very different things by "planning"; and such differences if not understood can lead to endless confusion. At certain stages of the development of a group it is very valuable to have an agreed formulation of the procedure to be carried out, so that members can make appropriate contributions.'

4

Open and closed situations

Reference has already been made to the fact that very early in their work together B.B.S. raised with Ralph Coverdale the distinction between open and closed problems. He said 'This was a topic that had interested me for some time. My interest began with my exasperation over an American view that in the modern world you don't have to be able to work things out; you need to know where to look to find the answers. This view links with recognizing the right answer when you see it and thence leads to reliance on true/false and multiple choice tests. I have a paper read by myself (first half) and P. Delin (second half) on open and closed. This was read to the Experimental Psychology Society in 1962. The ideas go back beyond that, probably to the mid-1950s when I was running the 11+ examination in one county. Ralph was excited when these ideas were put to him, and said "open situations! that's what managers face every day".'

In fact the distinction between open and closed became a cornerstone of Coverdale training very early in its development.

It may be helpful therefore to look at this distinction in more detail. It is clear that much of education is concerned with dealing with what may be described as closed situations, where problems are set and if the appropriate approach is adopted the solution may be deduced from available data. This tends to close people's minds and encourage a belief that in every situation it should be possible to state 'the problem' clearly and therefore find 'the solution'.

While in the real world this is so in some cases, many other situations are quite different in nature. Rarely are we given clear problems to solve. Something happens which presents a difficulty or opportunity, a new piece of information sets off a need, we receive an instruction, order or request. In many instances we do not have information readily available from our own experience to state a clear 'problem' and therefore define a solution.

It has been found useful to distinguish these differing situations by calling 'closed' those where enough information is available to define a solution. For example, in considering the situation it is possible to specify quickly what the end result will look like in fairly precise terms. Those where there is not sufficient information available are called 'open'.

Steps can be envisaged to close a situation down by narrowing requirements, or to open it up by widening categories of information to take into account; thus relative to 'Where can I buy today's *Daily Mail*?', the question 'Which newspaper should I buy and where?' is more open. It should be noted that the distinction open–closed is not the same as complex–simple (e.g. a closed situation may be complex to tackle); also that what appears open to one person may be regarded quite reasonably as closed to another i.e. the latter may, through past experience and existing knowledge, already be in possession of sufficient information to define a solution in precise terms.

The open–closed distinction has proved extremely valuable over the years for several reasons:

1 Originally it was customary to speak of open and closed problems, and with this went the use of the term 'solutions'. However, it has been found more useful to speak of open and closed situations and thus to avoid the terms 'problem' and 'solution'. A simple reason for so doing is that what one seeks to do is to find something to do in a situation, to make progress. On this view there is seldom initially an expectation that if one makes progress that is an end to the matter. Finding a way of getting oneself up out of bed in the morning is not designed to stop one having to do so in future, but to make the process easier or even more enjoyable. It has been said that managers do not solve any problem without creating a new, different one. Certainly it is true that the need to do things never ends and the current situation will be followed by the next and the next and so on. If one makes the assumption that in every situation it should be possible to state a clear problem and therefore find a solution it makes it difficult to get started and make progress when you find this is not so.

2 It raises the possibility, when faced with any situation, of opening it up or closing it down. If I observe that my garden is very untidy, I may close my task down to 'mow the grass' or open it

up to 'make it attractive to a prospective purchaser of my house'. The way in which a situation is opened up or closed down is by altering the aim (or rephrasing the task). This has the effect of changing the relevance of information, either increasing or diminishing the extent of relevant information. Deliberately focusing on a limited aim may mean that the information available relevant to the reformulated aim is such that the situation can now be seen as closed; in which case it is not then unreasonable to regard it as a 'closed problem' to which a solution may be sought.

3 It highlights the need for a difference in approach according to whether the situation is seen as closed or open. In open situations what is wanted is not a problem-solving approach but an orderly or systematic approach to getting things done which enables people to tackle the open situation and learn as they do so.

4 It becomes of immense importance where conflict arises between people. In tackling such situations the great limitation of problem-solving is that the parties may establish too definite a view of what they believe the solution should be (each purely from his own standpoint) before they have done sufficient real thinking or shared information and views about the matter in dispute. What is likely to be more fruitful is an approach aimed at moving forward and exploring possibilities, without any preconception as to what the outcome might be.

5

Decision theory and the turbine theory of action

In 1966 B.B.S. began to be concerned by the emphasis that was being laid by some people on the making of decisions. Elsewhere than in Coverdale much work and stress was centred on this step as being either the keystone in management, or the hallmark of an effective manager. He noted several points as relevant and important:

'1 While indecision can be disastrous, it is also clear that in the real world the making of a decision is not the same as undertaking a course of action. Who has not said, "I will do it tomorrow", and hasn't done it?

2 If progress is delayed until a decision is made, one consequence is that "makers of decisions" will tend to exaggerate their own importance and the work of others will be held up until the "great decision" is made.

3 "Decision" is not the same as "choice".

'Different situations can be envisaged. For instance, one may say that when there is a task, something to be tackled, information must be collected and sorted, one must then *decide* what is to be done, plan, act, review, etc. The decision becomes a central point and until it is made, planning and action cannot proceed.

'This is presenting one line of development in an extremely simple form. In some respects, a doctrine propounded by Ralph Coverdale favoured it, for he urged that once a proposal for a course of action had been made, the matter should not be discussed, but the proposal carried out. Decision is then not very important; if a proposal is made it is followed.

'This seems to suit an extreme situation where speed is all-important – something must be done without delay. But it seems to carry with it an implication that it will not matter if the action taken is unsuccessful, for one will be able to try again.

'Probably a more sophisticated approach would be to say: Collect the relevant information – (this implies that the task has been specified to some extent, for if there is no task, no information can be dismissed as irrelevant). On this approach, possible courses of action should be stated and considered and the probable consequences of each estimated.

'This approach in a computer-ridden world seems to offer security and objectivity, but the pitfall is provided by the "probable consequences" of courses of action referred to above, as can be seen when one considers "how is the probability estimated?" As this method almost certainly involves mathematical expressions, it carries great prestige.

'Clearly, however, this approach is liable to produce a situation in which choice must be exercised. Choice of a course of action is not the same as a decision to follow it. As Ralph Coverdale forcibly pointed out to a group who had been invited to back a winner, "choosing a winner is not the same as putting your money on it."

'A third account differs in important respects. As I have not yet succeeded in formulating it to my satisfaction, what follows is quite simply my latest account of what I have called a Turbine theory of action, in contrast with other methods emphasizing decisions, which I have described as Reciprocating Engine theories.

'In RE theories, one can regard work on a particular issue as falling into two phases, first the phase of collecting information, sorting it and planning i.e. considering resources and possibilities, which is separated from the phases of action and review by the *decision*. In the RE theory, these two phases correspond to the injection and compression of gas, separated from the expansion and exhaustion by the moment of explosion. Without the explosion, the machine doesn't work, hence by analogy the decision is essential.

'The Turbine theory requires an important difference to be made in one's view. Purpose' (which in an early attempt to classify 'aims' had come at the end of a scale of aims, objectives, targets etc. – a sort of longer term or ultimate aim) 'is here seen as different in kind. Purpose is now to be regarded as a form of energy. It is in this view somewhat like gravity, but it can take different forms. Purpose may be found in seeking power or riches or in love or hate. Aims, objectives, targets arise when purpose is directed and harnessed. Purpose of itself doesn't get things done but, with a systematic approach as an engine, things may be done.

'It seems to follow that, with this approach, decisions are no longer the great divide between preparation and action. I suggest that with steadfast purpose action will follow in good time, the relevant information must be collected, sorted and out of this will follow not a decision but a recognition or statement of what has to be done. Once the statement has been made, planning can follow and plans can be put into action and so on.

'Careful examination of this model will show that decision, removed from a central position as the pivot on which all turns, or as the explosion which drives a reciprocating engine, is in fact present throughout. One must decide what information is relevant, one must decide how to sort and organize information, at what point to make precise "What has to be done". One will have to decide who is available, what resources are available, and what modifications are needed in a plan as it is put into action. Thus, metaphorically, purpose supplying the driving force throughout requires decisions to "ignite".'

Thus in contrast to the Reciprocating Engine model, where the drive comes from the decision and everything turns on the *big decision* being made assuming the various possibilities, in the Turbine model power is derived from purpose and we have a continuous flow of little decisions. It seems, therefore, particularly appropriate as a model of a system for tackling open situations.

6

Problem solving and a systematic approach

As information about work in groups grew and the applications of a systematic approach were studied, attempts were made to classify what was observed. From this activity there emerged what became known as a number of 'themes', in other words classes of behaviour that are liable to appear when a group is at work. Between them they represent a range of topics which have at one time or another been seen as important and around which a body of observation and generalization collected. While B.B.S. was not responsible for the classification and the number of themes was never sacrosanct, some six or seven became well established and were found useful as topics for development with participants on courses. Those which were regarded commonly as established themes were observation, aims, process planning, listening and support, skills, authority, and systematic approach – which started to be seen as one theme of the training rather than the whole approach or system.

As described in Chapter 3 there had been a lot of work leading up to the promulgation in 1965 of 'A Systematic Approach' (see Appendix 1). This had developed out of the situation:

1 It was devised for businessmen (primarily for middle management).
2 It was built on the foundation of the value of action for the establishment of a group.
3 The concept of cycling as it developed led to B.B.S. thinking of the whole as a system driven round by an engine of some sort. Here he found himself reacting against the current doctrine that the thing that really mattered was the decision and saw the cyclic action as being powered by purpose.

4 Related to points 2 and 3 was Ralph Coverdale's emphasis on acting on proposals rather than seeking to collect and compare several. This led to the doctrine of putting into effect the first relevant proposal (which in turn had consequences in the form of a doctrine of 'support'). B.B.S. saw the situation from a somewhat different standpoint and stressed the point of collecting information and processing it in relation to aims, and also of moving forward as soon as there was enough information to see what had to be done.

Thus at that stage what had developed (as the whole system or approach) had characteristics which distinguished it as a method from problem solving, as for instance set out by Kepner Tregoe. First, it showed the value of action, of actually doing things together, as opposed to contemplation or discussion as a means of developing a team. Second, it was designed for getting things done rather than for finding things out. Third, there was the emphasis on the optimum use of time. Fourth, it was designed to be of value in open situations. Fifth, it incorporated the Turbine model which makes purpose the driving force and does not give the decision the outstanding position as in other methods.

Subsequently, in parallel with an increasing tendency to regard a systematic approach as one important theme, concerned largely with such issues as ordering an individual's thought and action and with coordinating the thinking and action of people in a group, a number of things happened which complicated the relationship between it and problem solving. It was, not surprisingly, found that if one collected more information one got a fuller view of the situation. The concepts of opening situations up and closing situations down were introduced as was the concept of setting criteria for judging success.

The emphasis on collecting information, on setting success criteria and the practice of closing down situations all tended to make the method, when regarded as but one of several themes, one of dealing with closed situations, and so a method of problem solving. However it is only if seen in this way and when applied to a situation which has already been closed down that a systematic approach can be described legitimately as a problem-solving method.

7

Learning styles and a systematic approach

'A systematic approach to getting things done' was seen when originally developed as, among other things, a programme of learning from experience, because it included review of performance and so allowed for later attempts to be tackled more effectively.

Over recent years much work has been done and much written about how people learn. In addition it has been suggested that individuals tend to favour one or more different approaches or 'styles' e.g. learning by doing, cognitive learning, imitation learning. In particular, work done by Kolb and others in the United States suggested a four-stage cyclic system of learning (concrete experience, observation and reflection, formation of concepts and generalizations, experimentation or testing of implications in new situations) where individuals naturally tended to emphasize one or more stages more than others.

B.B.S. observed (in a letter written in 1983) that 'Recently reading a work on learning styles I have been struck by noticing how close some of it comes to using stages which with very little change of name constitute a systematic approach to getting things done. I think this means that there is no need to look for different styles for different people, if, whatever they tackle, they set about it in terms of a systematic approach. One point, missed I think in the usual presentation, is that review of action entails observation, and presumably review is hampered unless action is observed well, so that the details and effects of action can be usefully considered. This aspect is glossed over if one says "action-review".' In another letter he commented how he had been struck 'by the close resemblance between a systematic approach and Kolb's cyclic system for learning. I hear that the latter is catching on. It seems to me highly frustrating that Coverdale has been doing what he is talking about since 1965 without putting it in so many words that if you attack something applying a systematic approach you do, in fact, learn. Here we meet a very interesting example of the principle that what matters is to get things done. I am fairly sure that Kolb *et al.* are concerned with the process of learning and have missed the points (a) that you learn when you get things done, following a systematic approach, and (b) that it is seldom indeed that one learns in one cycle and must continue cycling to produce the improvement that shows learning to be taking place.'

As early as 1963, during the development of a systematic approach, B.B.S. wrote to Ralph Coverdale about an article 'The Case for the Case Study Method' by Professor Pearson Hunt. He commented 'This article sets out in considerable detail the practice and theory, the merits and difficulties of the case study method as applied at the Harvard Business School. Since there is discussion in progress about the desirability of introducing similar methods into this country, it is of value to have such a clear presentation of the Harvard method.

'In his discussion of difficulties Professor Hunt makes no mention of what seems to me the most obvious and most serious. I deduce from this that he is not aware of it.

'The ultimate aim may be the production of good businessmen; but the proximate aim is given as the development of "judgement".

'You will see, as well as I can, when you read the article that the system firmly founded on Dewey's principle, is admirable as far as it goes. The evidence in a problem is reviewed, one decides whether more is needed, whether it can be obtained in the time available, one weighs the evidence where there is internal incompatibility and then one eventually reaches a decision as to what will happen or what should be done. It is all settled by discussion, no student ever has to *do* anything. No plan is ever put into action, there are no effects of action to be observed and so the implications of action can never be brought into the picture as fresh evidence, on which a fresh plan and fresh action can be based. The method takes no account of the need for action or of what can be learned from the results of one's actions.

'You have long stressed the importance of action and the need for follow-up and feedback; nothing makes this clearer than Pearson Hunt's article, if you read it with the point in mind.

'I believe it would be a major set-back for this country, if the Harvard Case Study methods were to be adopted in the form described in the *Cambridge Review*.

'To mount my hobby horse this is a beautiful example of the principle of indirection. It is very reasonable to insist that businessmen need to learn to deal with problems. It is easily seen that good businessmen have good judgement. The inference has been drawn that by developing good judgement one will produce good businessmen. What has been missed is that judgement is a phase in a continuous recurring process of observation, plan, action, assessment, replan etc. Judgement is only of value when developed in the setting of such recurrence.'

It is clear that when people do follow a systematic approach they move from insight or discovery with repeated experience to understanding and, with practice, to increased skill. They are also in a position over a period of time to:

1 Identify general lessons or 'rules of thumb' for themselves.
2 Elicit sound principles on which to base their future actions.
3 Develop their own conceptual framework.
4 Distil their own philosophy or set of values.

However, it is also clear from experience with large numbers of groups on courses that, while some people can elicit principles quite readily and may go on to develop their own conceptual framework and philosophy, others seem unable to do so.

As B.B.S. has commented 'Underlying all that has been done there has been a principle that it is important for an individual to realize his or her potential and become more effective. Permeating it has been the concept that when people work together misunderstandings will arise unless there is common agreement and acceptance of what is done. Hence statements are made and recorded about practices to be carried out by a group.

'If these practices are carried out without understanding they become what I call ritual. There are several reasons why people will continue to carry out a ritual without understanding it. They may be very biddable; they may not want to delay others; they may not want to seem stupid; they may feel that in due course the meaning will become clear; they may just have the dim conviction that it is the proper thing to do.

'Ritual, if carried out in the appropriate situation, can produce results; the difficulty is to decide when it is appropriate or when it ceases to be appropriate.

'When courses of action, or practices, or plans are adopted by a group during a course, those who do so with understanding of the principles on which they are devised can see what variations are permissible or useful. Some who adopt a ritual may, by repeating it come in the end to understand the underlying principles; that is it comes to have meaning for them. Some, however, can learn a ritual and carry it out, but never go further, and are at a disadvantage if circumstances change or the ritual is departed from. To put it in another way, some have rule of thumb as their limit, some use rule of thumb as a way of comprehension of principles and some do not need rule of thumb at all because they can grasp principles from the first and see how they apply.'

While it is usually regarded as intellectually more creditable to be able to learn from principles from the start, it is clear and should be stressed that many very able and competent managers fall into the second category.

8

Action learning and a systematic approach

In 1979 B.B.S.'s attention was drawn to an article by R. W. Revans 'The Nature of Action Learning' (*Management Education and Development*, vol. 10, part 1, Spring 1979, pp. 3–23). In commenting on the contents he wrote:

'What Revans has to say is important and there are features of his system that the Coverdale Organisation should take note of. Note that I don't say imitate or adopt.

'The first point is that if a person produces a new system it is essential to look at what their aims are. When we start on this task it is worth distinguishing (a) the explicit aims, (b) circumstances which may point to implicit aims, (c) ideas accruing later which may approach the category of aims.

'With Coverdale and Revans the chief difference in (a) is to be seen in the titles, with the former's emphasis on action, 'getting things done', the latter's on learning, 'learning by doing'. Coverdale appears to work on the basis that if you do things you can learn from what you do (note his emphasis on the view that such learning will not just happen, you have to take conscious steps to ensure that it does). Revans appears to be saying that the important thing is to learn, and that this is best achieved by doing (with an assumption that if you learn your performance will improve). Also see the end of page 6 in the article, "Action learning is to suggest courses of action . . ." not, it seems, to do things.

'For (b) I would look at the circumstances in which they operated and their past histories. Coverdale was concerned that managers were being promoted for technical skills; and because he was operating in middle management the method he devised was most appropriate at that level – a level at which taking a fresh look at yourself was particularly valuable. Revans, by the mid-1950s, was a Professor having held posts of considerable seniority. He seems always to have been able to operate with men at the top and his ideas seem to me to be most appropriate there. (How well they work is another matter.)

'Moving to (c), in the course of development many interesting and valuable ideas have turned up. I don't think that when Coverdale began he had seen the important effects of courses being designed round small groups i.e. teamwork. I don't think he had appreciated the importance of aims. "The choice to help" came later. One could extend the list. In Revans the most striking examples for me are the questions "What is an honest person?" and "How do I become one?" These were not in Revans' original design and they were not his questions, but he saw how important they were.

'The upshot of all this seems to be that while you are operating in situations like those Coverdale began with, continue to develop Coverdale methods, but watch to see what changes and developments are needed as you move into other fields. For instance, with middle management the inductive method and a fresh look at oneself are of enormous value, on the basis that when in middle management on the verge of promotion you want to review what you have been doing. Have you established good habits or are your methods holding you back? But for newcomers to industry, for instance, the same features are much less appropriate. They are moving into a fresh situation and need to familiarize themselves with existing and proven methods.

'What I have said here about Coverdale and Revans applies *mutatis mutandis* to other methods which one hears about.'

9

Observation

The importance of observation has been stressed in one form or other from the very beginning of the work involving those ideas which are the subject of this book. Initially this can be seen in the inclusion on the first courses of demonstrations, where the fallibility of human report and the great differences between individuals of what they report having observed were brought out. Attempts to cope with these features of report highlighted the importance of comparing the observations made and establishing common comprehension among people.

Ralph Coverdale saw the value to a group of having a detached 'observer' ('the spectator sees most of the game') and the value to an individual member of a group of the opportunity of being an observer, since activities and people look different according to whether you are participating in 'an activity' or watching it. Observers were instructed to observe and report to the group on matters relating to the process of carrying out a task. However, it became apparent that most found this very difficult and so the question of how to observe was raised. In considering this question B.B.S. notes that he began to study more closely the reports which were being made. He continues 'I found that early reports were narratives of the sequence of events, chiefly in terms of what this or that person had said, and also that this was precisely the form of report which I should have had to make had I been called on to make one. This was to some extent chastening, but at the same time confirmed my view that it was not so easy to make penetrating observations as one might suppose.

'I felt that I would have been able to supplement what had been said, and I could on occasion do so, but even then I was aware that if I had been called on to explain to the group the processes of interaction which were unfolding before me, I would have been hard put to do so.

'This stage was succeeded by another where I began to notice the behaviour of individuals, and about the same time noticed that reports by observers included comment on fellow members, though this carried little hint that the observers could interpret what they had observed. In several groups when this happened such comment was not received passively by the syndicate as a whole – accusations were made on occasion that the observer was not speaking for the syndicate but giving his own or a biased report. Several times this reached a point when the syndicate arranged for their observer to say "nothing to report" when it was obvious to one present at their proceedings that the whole syndicate was in a state of flux with unresolved tensions between them. I have seen groups come through this phase to another where they can allow their observer to report freely to others on their proceedings, content apparently that any of them could present developments in a way the others could accept.'

This progression seemed similar to the stages noticed in a laboratory situation where subjects were called on to make quantitative judgements of an unfamiliar kind in terms of a scale supplied to them. At first they floundered, said it was impossible, or that their responses were meaningless guesses. They then tried to apply some system, but this stage was followed by one where they made explicit *comparative* judgements among the stimuli which had been presented to them, and finally seemed to settle down to respond to the stimuli in terms of a framework they had built for themselves out of their perceptions and responses since the start of the procedure. 'I felt here was a paradigm of behaviour in an unfamiliar situation. Applying it to the task of observing it was possible to discern the initial stage of puzzlement as to what was going on – a state which is easily seen if someone starts to observe some activity which is already in progress. It is not difficult to see how natural it is to try to apply past experience to make sense of what is seen and heard.

'As the body of observation in the particular setting under review grows, so internal relationships begin to be appreciated, until the stage is reached where what is perceived is perceived in terms of the experience which has accumulated in this setting.'

Thus comment on an observed behaviour would normally only arise and be made when enough had been observed to allow comparisons to be made in terms of regularities or of changes which had been noticed. Comment does not lead directly to interpretation, thus one may note that someone seems unusually surly or cheerful without having the slightest idea why. The usual basis for interpretation is that some theory or other is brought to bear. Thus those who, for example, accept Freudian theory, can explain or interpret something which has happened in the light of that theory. However, their interpretation may well not be agreed with by those who do not accept that theory or who subscribe to different theories.

There is an alternative basis for interpretation which does not present this difficulty. That is to bring the observed behaviour into relationship with other known facts. Thus one may not need to seek further afield for an explanation of unusual surliness should you know of some earlier private disappointment suffered by the person concerned. Where people share experience it becomes possible for them to agree about interpretation based on accumulated experience that they have shared.

At this stage in his consideration of the question B.B.S. recalled that in the Binet test there is an item, used at several age levels, in which the subject is asked to talk about a picture. 'Three pictures are shown to the subject with the instruction, "Tell me what you see in this picture", and the responses are scored according to the form they take. Responses in the form of enumeration of objects in the picture are regarded as appropriate to a three-year level. Description of the objects and their relationships (What is this picture about?, What is this a picture of?) is set at the seven-year level. (*Note:* It would ruin the test to say "Tell me everything you see in this picture", for this form of question tends to provoke the enumeration response even with intelligent children of this age.) Interpretation in terms of action ("Tell me what this picture is about") comes higher, and interpretation in terms of purpose higher still, being rated as appropriate to the twelve-year level.'

He pointed out that putting together his observations made on the courses with those made in the psychological laboratory and the above features of the Binet test, it was possible to say that, given an unfamiliar situation to report on, an observer begins by going down to or falling back on the level of enumeration i.e. a narrative is given of events in succession (as one finds for example in *Hansard*). At this stage any interpretation attempted in terms of the observer's past experience may well turn out to be mistaken. As acquaintance with the situation is built up, so patterns of behaviour, regularities of behaviour, and changes begin to be perceived. Reports become more descriptive, adding to the narrative of what was said some description of what was done and how it was done. These are succeeded by comment where the observer introduces his opinions (e.g. X spoke angrily) and starts to interpret, giving cause and effect in the light of principles he has begun to find. As interpretations these may be rejected by other members of the syndicate who do not accept these principles. Finally, as a body of common experience is built up, interpretations tend to be accepted by all concerned.

10

Improving observation

With the discontinuance of 'demonstrations', observation came to be valued on courses as the source of evidence about activities and behaviour in groups and hence as the basis for ideas about skills and resources; hence it was essential in the process of getting to know people on which is founded the development of mutual understanding and confidence in a group. In view of the difficulties noted in Chapter 9 both of observing and of conveying observations to others so that they are accepted, from time to time in Coverdale work interest has centred on training people to observe and on methods of observation. It is doubtful whether any of this improves the functioning of the special senses through which we actually take in selected features of our environment. What it certainly can affect is the control and direction of processes of search (for instance what one looks for is different if one is interested in what people wear or in what they eat) and these can in turn affect the kind of inferences drawn from observations.

Here it may be useful to point out that a number of observational systems have been devised by others for recording the proceedings of groups. Some are elaborate, requiring the use of a high standard of expertise by observers in recognizing and classifying events and evidence of inter-relationship as they witness them. Others are simpler, providing for example a list of behaviours exhibited by individuals to look for and record as they are noticed. From the material produced by using such systems, statements may be made about relative frequencies, about recurrences and changes, and about associations or conjunctions. However, any theories developed from the material must always suffer from the defect of being indifferent to whatever has been omitted in the process of classification, however exhaustive the system of classification may be.

In one interesting effort to focus on learning to improve methods of observation, B.B.S. set out to devise a fresh method. He reported subsequently:

'If I can speak of a usual method for myself of observing a group in action, I can describe it as trying to follow and understand what is going on, taking what notes I can to record the gist of affairs and things done or said that seem important.

'In this case I proceeded differently and began by recording something relatively trivial, but simple to record, in fact the source of spoken interventions by the members of a group over a period of time. As I have found in the past, such a tabulation sets up a pattern of intervention or contribution and, after a few minutes, tabulation need not be continued; because, for some time, one can hold the pattern in mind and notice changes.

'It is easily seen that the amount of information in this particular statistical record is not great, there are many other things about the proceedings of a group that one would wish to know. In a second trial I arranged my recording to move steadily across a sheet of paper, so that my record looked something like a musical score, thus producing a rough time record of contributions not merely a histogram as in the first case. I then found it possible to add, in making the record, something of the nature of a participant's contribution; e.g. whether it was a statement or a question etc. It also began to be possible, to some extent, to include marks to indicate non-verbal contributions made by members of the group.

'Doing this and reviewing at intervals I found that I began to form impressions of the group members, e.g. whether a man was usually silent but made useful contributions when he did intervene, or was mostly silent but in his rare spoken words only made trivial contributions. The inferences I drew from these trials were:

1 The device of beginning by recording something very simple, and of fairly high frequency of occurrence is useful. One reason for its usefulness is that a statistical pattern emerges fairly quickly, another that for the moment the task of observing is enormously simplified.
2 The very simplicity of the first trial allows and encourages the observer to see that more information can be recorded, so that a more complex record can be attempted.
3 There was clear evidence of improving skill in making such a record.
4 At first, being absorbed in the making of the record, I ended a

session with no idea as to what had been happening; but as skill improved, impressions began to form about the participants and what they were doing.

5 A distinct advantage of the method is that it is open to anyone to start where they like, i.e. with whatever phenomenon they find of interest to record.

6 Improvement in observation will come about through better organization of information.'

It was during discussions between B.B.S. and the co-author of this book about the development of this method that the latter commented on how it seemed to deal with *individuals*, that in the courses we were running our concern was with *incidents* and that, by implication, he was surprised by the approach B.B.S. had taken. The reason for the comment was that on Coverdale courses we had long been accustomed in review periods to encouraging groups to try to identify from their own observations significant incidents when progress had been made or difficulty had occurred, to suggest possible underlying causes, to propose what had to be done in future to carry forward and to extend causes of success and to overcome causes of difficulty, and to lay plans to implement those proposals. Indeed a commonly used procedure during process reviews was to work through a four-column chart (observation, interpretation, what has to be done, plan). Thus it was assumed that any improved method of observation would focus directly on identifying significant incidents. In examining this point B.B.S. quoted an incident from the course he had observed. It occurred during a working group session on a task where three 'steerers' had been given time together to consider the task in advance of being joined by three others ('joiners') who would work with them to carry it through to completion. 'Shortly after the full working party had come together and begun to work one of the joiners rose and said "It is important that we understand the meaning of the instruction given to us."

'I have no doubt that this intervention had a beneficial effect on the work of the group. (I made a note at the time that the tone of the group's work changed.) Understanding the meaning of the instruction led the group to see more clearly what to do. The treatment of 'incidents' in current Coverdale practice is to proceed to discover what was the underlying cause, to state what needs to be done and to make a plan for doing it. In the case quoted the three steps could be that the speaker was frustrated at finding that the steerers had not produced evidence of having considered the meaning of the instruction; what needs to be done in such a case is to explore the meaning of the instruction; and a reasonable plan for doing so is to secure two or more independent interpretations of the instructions received, to ensure that any differences are considered and to aim at an agreed interpretation.

'At this level of observation and review the incident and the review have been dealt with, but what is the position if one is concerned to improve observation? One line of attack is to say that more information is required. In fact more information can be supplied.'

At this point in his notes B.B.S. goes on to provide a much fuller description of events – how the steerers had talked about the task to little purpose, partly because no attempt was made to consider the meaning of the instruction, partly because of time devoted to the ideas of one of the three who came from Finland and whose contribution, drawn from an entirely foreign background was not understood by the others; how at this stage they had been joined by the three joiners, one of whom took the lead in trying to clarify the work the steerers had done; how this particular joiner, when the steerers were floundering, had slammed down and gone for the meaning of terms with common sense; how a second joiner, who had been chatting quietly to the steerer from Finland intervened soon afterwards to take charge to develop on a chart an intelligible presentation converting the Finnish steerer's ideas (which others in the group had failed to understand but which he had taken the trouble to listen to and comprehend) into terms that the rest could grasp. In addition he describes another incident in detail later in the same course during a completely different activity but where the actual incident involved one person who had been a steerer and one a joiner in the first. In this second incident the latter's apparently reasonable request to do something was refused by the former. While puzzling in isolation, the incident, if taken in conjunction with the earlier one, could be seen as a very interesting turning of the tables – or restoring the balance – between the two individuals. In the former, one had, as a joiner, rejected the work of the steerers led by the other; then in the latter case the other had reasserted himself, in which case the two incidents taken together seem more meaningful than the two taken independently.

B.B.S. pointed out that whether the interpretation was correct or not it was clear that the detailed observations he had been able to add produced a more meaningful body of information than the original version of the incident. This, coupled with many other observations, points to the conclusion that the richer the observation the more meaningful the incident becomes.

However, what is significant on further consideration is that the statements given above, as those of a four-column analysis, are not altered when the more extended account is known. The crucial information leading to what has to be done and a plan was already included in the initial impersonal statement of the incident. The original base statement led to a procedural plan, which still remains valid when other information is added. Thus the original statement included all the relevant information about procedure; the extra information is concerned with personal skills and with personal relationships. It is different in kind. This line of argument points to there being distinct aspects of review – procedural issues and matters concerning personal skills and interpersonal relationships. One probable effect of improving observation is likely to be to increase the volume of material noted relevant to the latter relative to the material concerning procedures.

It is also clear that by 'improving observation' we do not just mean making *more* information available but making *better* information available. Here B.B.S. commented that he could not produce a rigorous argument but that the following line of thought offered at least a plausible route to progress.

'In relation to what went on in the working group' (as referred to above) 'I could give even more detail from my notes, but it remains clear that the incident as it stayed in my mind turned on how the particular joiner spoke emphatically at a certain stage, going for the meaning of the wording of the instruction, and the effect on the group of his doing so. If we find that ancillary detail does not alter the findings of a "four-column chart", then it looks as if my personal processing or selection of information led me to report what was *crucial*. It may be then that what leads to improved observation is the development of a skill, the skill of being able to process, sort or select information so that what is reported contains or constitutes the essence of what is being observed.

'I think the most important implication of these views is that a way to improve one's observation is by understanding what is observed and so being able to select and report the most relevant features. To put it another way, what should be sought is not fuller, or more extensive, or more detailed observation, but better observation in the sense that it is more understanding, more comprehensive or more penetrating.'

While, as suggested earlier, it is doubtful whether it is possible to improve the functioning of the special senses themselves by training people to observe or by devising methods of observation for them to apply, it may well be that they can develop their skill in processing, sorting or selecting information so that they can provide 'better' observation in this last sense through practice, experience and self-monitoring.

Finally, there is another aspect of observation that seems to call for fuller appreciation. This is the developmental sequence of observation itself. The first stage of this is where observation is seen as a skill in itself, a second where the experience of observing constitutes the 'input' side of a feedback circuit, action taken as a result being the 'output' side. Many such feedback circuits are involved in our adaptation to our circumstances and one may concentrate on any or several. Beyond this stage, however, one may look further to our overall adaptation and seek to improve that, which will necessarily involve a variety of feedback circuits in coordination. When this is achieved observation becomes one aspect of an overall system of controlling adaptation. There are parallels in this picture with stages of reading, from the simple skill of deriving words from symbols, to the use of the skill of reading to obtain information, to reading being one aspect of our adaptation to our environment and our control of our activities.

11

Purpose and choice

The contents of this chapter are drawn substantially from a chapter under the same title by B. Babington Smith in Whiteley D. E. H. and Martin R. (eds) *Sociology, Theology and Conflict*, Basil Blackwell, 1969.

The terms 'purpose' and 'choice' carry overtones of philosophical argument about predestination and free will. Space precludes any real discussion of these arguments in this book, but one or two important aspects must be pointed out here. The whole of this chapter is written from the point of view of one who accepts free will and holds that when choice of a course of action arises the outcome is not foreordained. This means that in advance of choice being made, the course of events is not certain or settled. It does not preclude the possibility of producing an account *after* the event in terms of cause and effect. However, it must be recognized that only in a trivial sense is such an account an explanation of the course of events.

There are many people, however, who do not accept such a view. For determinists, as they are usually called, it is in principle possible to determine causal influences in advance and so predict what will happen. Where this occurs, as in many inanimate events, the outcome is regarded as having been explained. While a determinist may use terms such as purpose, choice, intention and aim, the implications of the terms may be entirely different from when the same terms are used by people accepting free will. This appears to be very marked in relation to purpose and aim. For a determinist the former seems to mean little more than the direction in which things are going, and it is hard to see that aim can mean anything else.

Those accepting free will seem to use the term 'purpose' commonly in two ways. One context is that of an objective, often long term e.g. 'For what purpose are you writing that book?' i.e.

what are you trying to achieve in writing it?, What is it to be used for? A second context, and the one in which it is used in the Turbine Theory of Action is that of a form of energy or a vector in that it has magnitude and a general direction. It may be shallow or deep and profound, fleeting or firm and unshakeable, superficial or underlying. It may be found in seeking power or riches or in love or hate. Aims, objectives, goals and targets arise when purpose is directed and harnessed.

Having attempted to make clear the position and viewpoint from which this chapter is written, what is of great relevance and importance for a manager is to highlight ways in which ordinary people's outlooks (and consequently their ideas and behaviour) differ and not just those of philosophers. For sooner rather than later in getting things done we have to deal with our fellows. In these dealings it helps for each to understand the other's outlook. What is perhaps the key point is brought out well in the following parable: Once upon a time there were three men in a railway carriage. The first sat with his back to the engine watching the trees and fields receding into the distance and thinking about the course of events which had brought him where he was. The second, facing the engine, saw the landscape grow and flash by while he considered the object of his journey and what he was going to do. The third man said, 'This is a very comfortable compartment; it is very gratifying to travel first class.'

The three men in the parable are Freud, Jung and Adler. While the parable could be expanded to bring in allusions to all sorts of features of their teaching this is enough to make the point. Outlook in time offers a crucial basis for comparison between these three great psychotherapists.

Freud, travelling with his back to the engine looks to the past. The future is out of sight behind him. Using a concept usually known as 'figure-ground', the past is the 'figure' for him; the future and all concerned with it is in the 'ground'. Now instincts are forward-looking, so for Freud they and their influence are not in the 'figure', but in the 'ground'. The term which Freud used for this situation of being 'out of sight' or 'in the ground' has been translated as 'unconscious'. Freud was explicitly concerned to find out how a patient had come to his present state, and it was explicitly (at any rate at one stage) his doctrine that the acceptance by the patient of the origins of his condition, as they were recovered by the process of psychoanalysis, constituted the cure.

Jung travelling with his face to the engine looks to what is ahead; the past is behind him. So for Jung purpose is explicit, it is in the 'figure', and it is conscious; but the past history stretches behind out of sight and, using the 'figure-ground' principle again, is in the unconscious. If we think of ways in which we now function as having developed through the past history of the race, i.e. that we inherit not only our physical body but also its functioning, and the ways in which it can function because of its construction, then these will, for the Jungian, be 'in the ground' and 'out of the figure', that is, out of consciousness. These ways of functioning give the 'archetypes' which influence our thinking and in terms of which we think, and are to a great extent shared with our fellows.

Adler was concerned with adaptation to present circumstance, and realization of the lifestyle of the person, as a means to power.

Thus the contrast drawn here at the conscious level is between Freud's concern with cause and explanation, Jung's with purpose and meaning and Adler's with power and adaptation. As a useful oversimplification, it can be said that Freud was concerned to trace the origin of trouble and believed that realization and acceptance constituted the cure: 'The more fully the causal reason underlying a state is revealed the more fully is it explained.' To a non-Freudian it seems that patients may feel enormously relieved by Freudian treatment, but they do not know what to do next, and the old sequence is likely to happen again. Jung was concerned with purpose and meaning, but, to the extent that Jung is dealing with the future, his answers cannot be given in terms of fact; and anyone involved in this system must come to terms with the use of symbols and principles. Adler was concerned with inferiority complexes, with compensation for defects, and the will to power. These are all valuable concepts, but what was the power for? He has no answer, any more than to the question, what is adaptation for?

Proponents of each of the three schools of thought were concerned to argue that they were right and that the others were wrong. But once one has seen the relevance of the time relationships involved, the question of rightness or wrongness of the three positions shrinks in importance. It becomes comparable to the question as to which is the right way to see a reversible figure.

Among ordinary men you can find examples of the same three outlooks, and a viewpoint which makes good sense to one man may seem wilful perversion of experience to another. If such men can come to see the extent to which their differences arise from outlooks, understanding may be achieved, or even agreement.

In a discussion of the saying 'there are no bad pupils, only bad teachers', a scientifically-trained man was heard to assert firmly that the truth of this statement simply depended on the facts, and what were the facts? The view which prevailed and which he finally accepted, was that, whatever the facts, this would be a good motto for any teacher to hang upon his wall and that its complement 'there are no bad teachers, only bad pupils' might well be on every pupil's desk. In demanding the facts he was looking back to the past, while the acceptance of the saying as a guide is to face forward.

Matters might be simpler, of course, if everyone belonged to one or other of the three classes and either faced forward or backward or lived in the present. But life is not so simple, nor does the same person always behave in the same way; nor indeed is it contended here that they do – or even should! In fact, it is of the greatest importance to people to be able both to plan for the future and to analyse the past, and their life will be the poorer if they cannot at times lay aside care and criticism and enjoy themselves here and now.

Let us now turn more directly to the manager or indeed to anyone else who is concerned with getting things done in the future. If their outlook is to face the past and think in terms of cause and effect then when they reach the point of planning this becomes primarily a matter of considering the possible courses of action. Such a person must produce the possible sequences of events flowing from the present state. He or she may assess the value or desirability of the various possible outcomes, and it will be for someone to choose which to try to follow.

Someone with a mainly forward-facing outlook must adopt a different approach. If one 'faces the engine' one cannot deal in facts or events, but must accustom oneself to using symbols, principles and generalizations. On this basis planning takes on a distinctive character. Facing forwards one can state the principles or standards which will guide one's actions towards an objective. The resulting planning will be more like navigating by compass or stars than following an AA route.

If these two types of planning, both of which may be encountered in ordinary life, are typical of travelling with one's back to the engine or facing it respectively, what about the person whose concern is the present? It is suggested that for such people planning is uncongenial and unfamiliar. Among these are those who, when things go well, live for the present, but are liable to be overwhelmed in the expedients of 'crisis management' when things go wrong. By 'crisis management' is meant a state in which action is reaction to sudden and unexpected change. When there is no planning, all changes come as sudden and as unexpected.

In practice, of course, it may be advisable to have at one's disposal all three outlooks referred to above so that they may supplement each other. However, it is observable in everyday life that people who have developed one of the three methods described may not be aware of other possibilities and therefore seek to persuade others to follow their own example. In short, some individuals tend to face forwards and think, live and act in terms of purpose, others to face backwards and see life as an inevitable succession of effects of causes, others again to think in terms of observable concomitant variation.

What is said above is an attempt to illustrate what a difference it makes to one's outlook to face one way or another and to the meanings which one will attach to some very important terms. This theme assumes even more importance as soon as one person needs to deal with and have some form of transaction with another, and increasingly so as the numbers involved increase to three and beyond. Two or more people faced with a situation where something needs to be done may begin to argue about it. In such circumstances it is possible to ask, 'Why should something be done?' From experience it is clear that some people habitually understand 'why' as 'for what purpose', facing the future, while others, just as spontaneously, take it in the sense of 'for what reason', facing the past. Taking a simple example from managers attending training courses, an answer typical of the former is 'to improve my skill in managing', and one typical of the latter is 'because my boss sent me'. Realization of this difference in outlook helps two such people to understand each other better. However, where something needs to be done in the future both will need to face forward if they are to work together effectively. If they do face forward and compare their views on why (for what purpose) they need or wish to tackle the situation, their answers may still provoke argument. If so, they may need to ask why again to their initial answers and do so repeatedly until a level of generality is reached at which both can agree and a common basis for progress can be recognized. (This procedure or gambit was devised originally by Ralph Coverdale.) However, here another general point of importance can be made. People also differ widely in the timescales of their outlooks. Thus even when facing forward some give evidence of thinking much further into the future than others. As the questions go deeper different interests emerge: home, business prospects, national politics or the welfare of mankind. Perhaps, if the matter were fully explored, all of them would turn out to be in the picture, though the relative importance attached to home or business or country would vary from one man to another. Some will offer a basis on which two men or more could cooperate, such as the welfare of employees, or going deeper the welfare of the country (or going deeper still, as with the great powers of East and West, the survival of mankind). Other aims, admirable in themselves, such as welfare of an individual's spouse and children, attract sympathy but do not alone provide a basis for others to share efforts in achieving. One point still stands out clearly, that if we face forward there are possibilities of finding aims which we can agree to pursue. If we look back and face the past we may find resemblances, but, the further we pursue the chains of causation which resulted in our coming together, the more these chains will be seen to be distinct. While common suffering or common joy may be a basis for understanding and sympathy, they do not offer in themselves a basis for action. However, if people with such common backgrounds look forward, aims may be derived that two or more could agree upon. To know someone's history and reasons for their actions may help one to understand them. To know their aims enables one to hinder them or help them. The choice is always open.

12

Specifying aims

Faced with a situation where there is a need to do something, it is clear that what is to be done and how it is to be done will differ according to the direction in which, or the object at which, the activity is aimed. If one sets out to obtain a newspaper with the aim of updating oneself with the latest national news, presumably today's newspaper will be sought. If one needs it to light a fire, any paper would do – or indeed any suitable alternative. In practice it is very difficult to apply a systematic approach to getting something done without some specification of an aim or aims (however general or specific, broad or narrow, 'open' or 'closed'). The extent and nature of the information relevant will depend on the aim to be pursued. Without such specification no data can be dismissed as irrelevant; therefore it is not possible to gather and process *relevant* information.

People tend to specify aims for themselves through the answers to such questions as: Why do I need to tackle this situation?, What do I need to do it for?, What am I trying to achieve in tackling it? Once specified, aims can be seen as differing in a number of ways and being described by a number of words in common use. Thus target, goal, objective and end are all used for what is aimed at or sought – things to be achieved, aspirations to be realized. They may be things, places or states and in principle can be reached or achieved and specified as to nature, place in space and time, and often in terms of cost.

Aims may relate to home and family interests, to job and business prospects, to the local community or the nation, or to the welfare of mankind. With respect to time, they may need to be achieved short term, over an intermediate or longer term or as an ultimate. Any situation may be 'opened up' from an initial specification of an aim by asking 'why/what for?' to the stated aim and seeking a number of differing answers. If in turn one asks the same question to each answer and does so repeatedly, the answers will tend to become increasingly more general. Following such a procedure (which was devised originally by Ralph Coverdale) helps to set the immediate situation in a broader context and may open up the field of possibilities for action. The arrangement of aims which can be derived by following this procedure can be seen as analogous to a map from which a route may be selected and pursued. The relative importance attached to any particular tiers or chains of aims at any one time may vary. However, the effort of thinking more deeply about a situation and 'opening up' in this way facilitates conscious judgements on the extent of the information to be gathered and the relative importance to be given to different pieces of information in a particular situation. It cannot of course indicate the specific aims to pursue. That choice rests with the individuals and may be influenced by such factors as their assessment of the resources available, the risks involved, their own level of confidence and of aspiration. It is noticeable that many people seem uncomfortable when faced with 'open' situations and seek to 'close them down' by focusing very quickly on limited aims. Clarifying where these are intended to lead, through following a procedure like that outlined above, helps to ensure that this is not done without some consideration of wider issues.

Having selected one or more tiers or chains of aims to pursue, as progress is made through the stages of information gathering and processing, stating what has to be done, planning and implementing the necessary actions, keeping those aims in mind, observation of how the situation is changing and developing may lead to changing or modifying the aims. The Turbine Theory of Action provides a dynamic model envisaging continuing interaction between aims, method and observation, with the driving force provided by purpose.

Once aims are specified it also becomes possible to ask how success in achieving or progressing towards them may be judged. Thus criteria of success may be set to act as guidelines or marks by which to judge success in performance when the job is finished or at specified stages in its progress. In addition, specifications or standards may be established to act as guides to performance or to requirements in materials or manpower when the job is in progress. Further it may also be useful to establish in advance some indicators or signs to look for as pointers to, or evidence of, progress in a desired direction. Consideration of any of these questions during the preparation stages may help in the specification of what has to be done. For example, the statement that a jumbled up pile of playing cards will have been sorted out successfully, as a preliminary to possible use, when they are in number order within suits in separate packs makes what to do to sort them clearer. Similarly, the statement that one criterion of improvement in service to customers is that a response to any letter is despatched within two days indicates just one among many things to be done.

Just as the extent and nature of observation change as soon as more than one person becomes involved in an activity, so the concept of aims becomes more complex as soon as people need to interact with each other to get things done. For real progress efforts must be made to clarify the differing aims and the differing relative importance of each which individuals see as needing to be pursued in any situation. Establishing how differing statements of aims made by different people relate to each other is one important requisite for agreement on how to move forward.

13

Task and process – and the balance

The continued emphasis on action during the early stages in the development of what has come to be called Coverdale Training led, on courses, to groups being engaged in many tasks, which came to be distinguished as real, e.g. arranging a course dinner, or as artificial, e.g. 'sort these cards', or as simulated, e.g. a business game. For a period, courses opened with a business game which appeared to be a highly appropriate activity.

The importance of action in helping a group to form has already been commented on. The use of tasks also reflected Ralph Coverdale's concern that people should take the responsibility for their own actions (hence the need to do things not just plan them) and that managers should take responsibility for managing others and not just for the technical aspects of their work. The courses were not concerned with improving technical skills and therefore it was regarded as undesirable for participants to become too deeply involved at this stage in their level of achievement. The course was more concerned with the study of how to do things and with developing good ways of working together. These aims were frustrated where people became 'task mesmerized' and too deeply involved in the level of performance. This proved to be the case with business games. In them, strong competition developed between groups in a course, and some participants believed that they were learning how to do business. For these reasons business games, which had appeared to offer excellent opportunities for learning in a simulated situation, were found not to be appropriate and were abandoned.

The distinction between concern with 'how things are done' and 'what is done' was crystallized with the importation of the term 'process' for how things are done, particularly how human beings interact, leaving the term 'task' for what is done. So far as B.B.S. could discover, Ralph Coverdale owed acquaintance with the terms to meetings with Matthew Miles at the Steel Company of Wales in 1960 or 1961. In any activity one may distinguish the *task*, or what is done and the *process*, or how the task is done (i.e. all the various aspects of the way in which it is carried out).

The process may then be subdivided usefully into:

1 The means – equipment, tools, resources to be used.
2 The method – the way in which it is done, methods and procedures used.
3 The human interaction involved (where there are two or more
  people).

To give a simple example, we set the rubbish alight (task):

1 With matches and paraffin (means).
2 By sprinkling the paraffin on the rubbish and throwing a lighted
  rag onto the pile (method).
3 I dissuaded him from lighting the heap and then pouring paraffin on (human interaction).

This further subdivision of how a task is carried out highlights the need to clarify whether, when the term 'process' is used, it refers to human interaction only or to all aspects of 'how'.

B.B.S. has commented, 'There is no doubt in my mind that in the earliest days of Coverdale work the general tendency in commerce and industry was to consider performance in terms of material products. (Matters of human interaction were matters for person-nel departments not aspects of line management.) The value of small group work in showing that human relations are intrinsic to any situation and any job has been very great. And it is fair enough that small group work should be seen as giving an opportunity for the study of human relations and qualities, not for training people in technical skills. For a period interest concentrated on process, which allowed much to be learnt about human interaction and what were called "process skills".'

However, he also observed 'I am equally clear that within the Coverdale Organisation the emphasis on process got out of hand. I think Ralph Coverdale himself was quite largely responsible for this and much time had to elapse before it could be acknowledged that all activities among people involved task and process and that attempts to study process in isolation lead nowhere.'

There is also the point that, while it is important that people do take the opportunity on such a course to study how they interact, how they behave, what resources they have, rather than their performance (e.g. how high a tower they build), it is also important that they set themselves high standards and consider what to do if these are not reached. It is true that a lower standard of task achievement may be accepted temporarily while new methods and behaviours are tried and learnt. However, it is equally true that what is sought is interaction, behaviour, methods and use of resources that contribute to high-quality task performance, not just any results.

Another way of looking at the task–process distinction, which has at times been drawn very sharply and strictly in Coverdale work, is to see this separation as a teaching device, particularly useful in the early days when concern with process issues was so unfamiliar and there was warrant for dealing with them separately. However, it is essential that people's understanding is taken beyond this level and they are helped to see that in any situation both are involved and that they are inter-related. In trying to get things done it is not possible to consider *what* is being done in isolation from *how* it is being done, nor to consider *how* in isolation from *what*. The balance must be maintained through awareness of all aspects of *how* without losing sight of the details of *what*. Undue emphasis on either to the exclusion of the other leads to difficulties. As B.B.S. pointed out to Ralph Coverdale, 'You speak of the manager as having two quite separate problems.' (The management of his team and the operation of the latest technical information.) 'If you attempt to separate these aspects of management, the task will tend to fall apart. The function of management can be viewed from the standpoint of teamwork, it may also be viewed from the standpoint of its relationship to technical advances. The description of management in the two cases may be as different as could be the description of a Landseer by a painter or a zoologist.'

14

Assessing performance and talents

Early in the development of Coverdale Training, Ralph Coverdale introduced what later came to be called the Skills Exercise, to crystallize what the participants in a group had observed about each other and to exchange this information in a way which challenged hesitation and demanded frankness and acceptance of personal responsibility. In fact the name was misleading, since the exercise was concerned with assessing *performance* – what people had done – not their skills.

In writing to him during 1963 B.B.S. noted, 'The view that what students should aim at is assessing the talent of others and turning their talent to account is admirable. This is the most valuable and characteristic lesson they can learn from the courses you are running. At the same time it is probably the most difficult.

'The practical problem of ensuring that this lesson be learnt would be simplified if it were tackled in two stages. I propose that we look on Part 1 as giving a student the opportunity:

1 Of learning about the *formation of a team for a purpose.*
2 Of learning to look at oneself and how others see one.
3 Of seeing how one can contribute to the success of the team.
4 Of learning how to set about an open or closed problem (or situation).
5 Of being introduced to the various stages of observation.
6 Of being introduced to the study of process.

'Part 2 can then be seen more clearly as an opportunity of learning about:
1 The development of a group (which can tackle anything) as opposed to a team developed for a particular purpose.

2 The development of looking at others, i.e of talent assessment, to cover process skills as well as task skills.
3 The development of the concept of aiming to *help others* to contribute to the success of the group.
4 Tackling a process task; e.g. what to do if told to form a group, or to study planning or to go and enjoy oneself etc.

'By asking people to describe and assess themselves ("In what way did you help or hinder the operation of the group?") and to assess the others in their syndicate in relation to the same question we obtained material which was directly meaningful to those concerned, and they were helped to see themselves more clearly and to see themselves as others saw them.

'They had assessed people on *what they had done*. This procedure is not the same as assessing their own or others' *characteristics*. As a result the discussion was of what individuals had done and how they were seen by others, not of their roles or characters. The discussion of personality and of contributory roles in groups might well be deferred to Part 2 and the discussion in Part 1 be restricted to non-technical terms.'

In another note on the assessment of people and talents, B.B.S. wrote: 'Assessment must be related to time in the sense that with the lapse of time more evidence must become available (in the course of social intercourse) on which assessment can be based.

'It would be most interesting to develop this theme of assessment in this connection, and Ralph Coverdale has made the point that the assessments in the middle of a five-day course are more superficial than those in the middle of a fortnight's course.

'What can be done in a weekend?

'What can be done in an hour's interview?

'Is it worth considering that the crucial points are manifest immediately, that the lapse of time confuses the issue by giving varying amounts of evidence on the possible facets or features of a character, and that the only important change is in the kind of language used to formulate the assessment?

'Against this one may say that, of course, some quality like tenacity or obstinacy can only be discerned and assessed in terms of observation over a period of time, because it is essentially a quality which is related to behaviour over a period of time. In one instant a person can only be seen as being on your side or against you?

'It may well have been wise to restrict the question of assessment to positive qualities in a weekend course. Even on longer courses it may be that ways in which someone hindered can be turned to account: in fact this is almost an article of faith. But it seems to me that the question asked is better phrased factually "How did X help or hinder the operation of the group?", and then to see whether the principle or trait underlying the hindrance could have been converted to being helpful. In other words, the idea that tendencies can be seen either as negative or positive and that the one can be converted to the other is better introduced after some attempt has been made at assessment.'

15

The doctrine of success

At an early stage in the development of Coverdale Training B.B.S. raised the question of whether bafflement had a place in the courses. He commented that 'Two distinct theories of learning have to be considered; one is that nothing succeeds like success, that success reinforces a tendency and that nothing is gained by failing.

'The other view is that if you make no mistakes you make nothing. You learn from mistakes and the most effective way of learning is to meet something difficult and overcome it.

'Possibly the second is but a version of the first; in the sense that even the second theory requires success in overcoming difficulties. The big difference is that in the second view confusion and failure are acceptable in the early and intermediate stages, and even desirable, because it is only by way of these that a situation or process is understood. The weakness of the first approach is that it leaves the learner powerless in the face of any variation in the situation which makes an already learned process unsuitable. The argument in favour of the second view runs like this. We can never tell when we shall encounter an unfamiliar situation, let us therefore make the acquaintance of a variety of unfamiliar situations and study the internal processes which go with our attempts at solving or coping with them. If we can recognize the methods which were successful, and the experiences which went with them, we should know better how to tackle strange situations that we encounter later.

'As with observation, there is a sequence of experience or process which one goes through in a situation initially unfamiliar. When one has to do something about such a situation, there is initially a phase of confusion. The next stage is a series of attempts to employ methods from the past, i.e. to bring experience to bear. With repeated attempts relationships within the new situation begin to be appreciated, and thus fresh experience (i.e. experience relevant to the situation itself) is built up. As the system of internal relationships grows so one knows more and more about the situation until one acts "in terms of" it. This statement does not imply that one will have explained it, but that the series of one's acts will be internally consistent.'

However, as more courses were run B.B.S. notes that 'Ralph Coverdale observed that, if people are asked to comment on the work of others, their comments are almost always adverse. Coupling this with the known effect that people tend to grow and improve if praised, but to shrink and wither under continual blame or carping, he stressed the importance of noting what was well done and saying so directly to the people concerned.

'To many delegates on courses the effects of this, unfamiliar, emphasis on success were electrifying, it was something they had never met before.

'The concept of success spread to the assessment of "skills" in the form of "obstenacity"; a concept which ensures that the positive or favourable aspect of traits or skills (which at first sight seem unfavourable) is brought out, after which it may be possible to turn them to account.' (Thus what is described as 'obstinacy' may also be seen as 'tenacity'.)

'Great emphasis was laid on learning from success and it was held that from failure one only learns what not to do. Attention was concentrated on success and on spreading success and on learning the causes of success, to such an extent that failure ceased to be considered.

'In this instance emphasis on the importance of success as a key to improved morale diverted attention from seeing that "*success*" is of its nature a process term and that its complement in the job as a whole is *full* information which contains unpalatable as well as palatable matters. One result of this emphasis on success is to produce a very "bland" atmosphere where everything is praised or commended and nothing is criticized. Where this situation is accepted, the recipients can become very pleased with themselves and very complacent. For a thorough appreciation and understanding of a situation what is required is full information. One cannot reach a full understanding if some information is withheld.'

This illustrates very well how an idea, valuable in itself, (that of learning from and building on success), can become a stumbling block if not regularly submitted to review. It is so often found that people concern themselves first with failure or concentrate first on weakness that it is important to ensure that attention is paid to success and to strength, in order to counterbalance normally prevailing tendencies. However, if a due balance of attention to success and failure, to strength and weakness, is not subsequently set up and maintained, difficulties will arise.

'1 Since learning arises out of inferences based on observations, such inferences are best based on *all* information; it is inefficient to neglect any category.

2 While the morale of an individual or of a group can be affected adversely by lengthy analysis of failure, errors or mistakes, but positively by analysis of success or progress, both drawing lessons and working out what to do are best based on both.

3 Too great an emphasis on success can lead to the use of any time spent in reviewing performance being devoted to "success" to the exclusion of difficulties that can be much more deep-seated. If, for instance, by praise and encouragement I persuade someone to continue with an exhausting job to its completion, there is a simple implication that giving praise and encouragement are successful practices. However, there still also remains the possibility that review of the exhausting job would reveal defects in method and thence lead to redesign of the job to make it less exhausting. If my review concentrates on success and on spreading a method that surmounted a difficulty, I run the risk of dealing with that difficulty at a superficial level rather than treating it radically.

4 It is a matter of observation that people do tend to grow and improve if the success of their efforts is noticed and commented on directly to them, but wither under continual blame and carping. However, in reviewing someone's performance with them, full information will include both successes and difficulties or shortcomings. It is the way in which that information is presented and the way the review is conducted which has an effect on morale. This includes both the order of presentation and consideration of the material and the balance between success and failure.'

16

Steering and joining

The ideas contained in this chapter owe their origin to comments of participants on early Coverdale courses to the effect that, while the experience of trying to form a team was valuable, there were in practice very few teams in business. What happened day to day was that one had a series of meetings (or transactions) with different people, singly or in small groups, on different topics, and that in each instance what was necessary was to help that particular 'group' to get down to work quickly and get things done without the 'luxury' of forming a team. As a result a Part 2 course was developed which, among other things, gave the experience of working in groups of various sizes for short periods. In some instances participants were given tasks (to be carried out later by working parties) in advance of the full working parties coming together. They were told that they had a period of time to carry out whatever work they considered useful in advance of the meeting of the full working party. Those given the task came to be called 'steerers' (on the grounds that they would be expected to steer the full working party) and the others 'joiners'.

This particular situation was seen to be very similar to many of those experienced by people in their normal work. Thus managers could see that on some occasions they themselves had situations to tackle and had time to think about those situations before getting others to work with them in getting something done; on other occasions they found themselves in the position of 'joiners', being expected to work with others who had already had time to think about the situation.

It was seen as encompassing a rather wider range of circumstances than is generally conjured up by the terms 'leading' and 'following'. These tend to suggest that those leading have some seniority of position, whether through appointment or election, over those following. There are a great number of situations, even within organizations where there is a clear hierarchical structure, as is the case with most businesses, where one person needs to secure the cooperation of others who are neither accountable to them nor 'junior' in any way – managers dealing with their colleagues from other departments, staff specialists dealing with line managers, even managers with their bosses.

As more people attended courses and studied what happened in steering and joining activities a body of ideas came to be accumulated about such situations. For example, it became clear that where the steerers concentrated almost exclusively on the content of the task in their preparation, working out in detail not only what had to be achieved but what was to be done and how it was to be done in detail, those joining complained that they had no opportunity to contribute their ideas but were just being expected to 'do as they were told'. Conversely if the steerers gave little evidence of having thought clearly about the task and appeared to have done virtually nothing on it, the joiners felt that they should have been presented with more to build on. It was also observed that while the steerers could do much to make it possible for the joiners to contribute to the success of the working party in carrying out the task, joiners needed to get themselves involved. The effects of making this 'choice to help' were clear.

Situations which can be seen as 'steering and joining' abound within any organization, where the efforts of a number of people are required for things to be produced or services provided, even though they may carry out many of their activities independently. B.B.S. has suggested that it is useful to distinguish some differing situations where more than one person may be required. One case is where the task could be carried out by a single person but the time needed is not available. Then several people doing the same work may complete the task in the given time e.g. there are 500 envelopes to be addressed and despatched by this afternoon's post. A second is where the force or effort cannot be exerted by one person e.g. to lift a lorry off someone who has been knocked down. A third is where different types of skill or expertise are required and different operations may be needed at the same time or in concert, e.g. an orchestra.

In the first example it would appear only to be necessary to ensure that all are clear on the aims and criteria to be met, are prepared to help get the job done and have sufficient skill or competence in the work to do what is wanted. In the second some coordination will be needed between the operators which they may well provide for themselves, while in the third someone beyond the operators will probably be needed to organize and coordinate. It is true that the importance of the orchestral conductor's contribution during a performance is occasionally questioned (e.g. the story of the experienced member of a well-known symphony orchestra who replied, 'I didn't notice' when asked who had conducted a symphony they had just played). This may of course be an example of, 'Of the greatest leaders the people say "we did it ourselves"', but in any event one assumes that much of the organizing and coordinating will have been provided during the rehearsals!

Systematic preparation for getting something done where others are required can be seen as considering both the substance of the situation and how to communicate with others, how to ensure this has taken place, and how to encourage and enable others to contribute to the best of their ability. Such consideration also includes judging at what stage in one's own thinking to start involving those whose contribution is required.

If we take the three situations outlined above in turn, in the first the person with the job will need to take into account the level of competence and familiarity with the work of those whose assistance is sought as well as their likely willingness to help or level of commitment (again the importance of how well he or she knows them is clear). Both factors will influence the amount of detailed instruction he or she needs to provide in communicating and the amount of monitoring or supervision deemed necessary.

In the second additional thought will need also to be given to how the necessary coordination is to be provided.

In the third, which is by far the most common to managers within an organization, further issues arise related to organization and coordination including how the work is to be led or 'steered' and how those following or 'joining' can contribute effectively. Study of such situations suggests a number of additional principles, some applicable to 'steering' and some to 'joining'. Those which seem important to those steering are:

1 Preparing to steer involves consideration of both the content of the job to be tackled and how to make good use of the abilities of those joining i.e. the procedures to be adopted, the practices to

be used and the principles of behaviour to be kept in mind and followed.

2 Consideration of the content involves judging at what point in one's own thinking to start to communicate with those joining. The point here is that the further the steerer goes the less opportunity there may be for those joining to provide the relevant facts, experience and ideas they have to determining what is to be done and how to do it. Thus if the steerer has already worked out what is to be done and how to do it before communicating with the joiners, they will be put in a position of merely carrying out instructions and may well feel that their own ideas are not required or welcome. By contrast if the steerer begins to communicate at the point where it is clear what needs to be achieved in general terms and the criteria to be met but has gone no further in his or her own thinking, then those joining will be able to contribute the relevant information they have towards defining what has to be achieved more precisely, establishing what has to be done and planning how to do it.

3 Some factors which need to be taken into account in judging how far to go on the content of a job before involving the joiners are:

(a) The time available before there is an opportunity to communicate compared with that available for completing the job after that point.

(b) What the steerer knows of the skills, experience, knowledge, outlook, interests of those joining and their likely willingness to help and level of commitment to the aims being pursued.

(c) The balance between ensuring as good an outcome as possible on the particular job and encouraging contribution from those joining on that and future jobs e.g. in situations where there is a continuing relationship between steerer and joiners, as with a manager and own subordinates, the former may be particularly concerned to steer an activity in such a way that he or she encourages and coaches them in order to develop their willingness and ability to contribute in future.

4 Consideration of how to steer also involves being clear on the methods or procedures to be adopted to:

(a) Ensure the joiners have a common understanding of: the situation; the aims to be pursued; the sort of outcome and quality required; and any other relevant thinking or work already done by the steerer.

(b) Gather and process relevant information including facts, experience and ideas from those joining.

(c) Establish and ensure common understanding of: what has to be done and the priorities; and plans for doing so, at least to the extent of *who* is to do *what* by *when*, even though the detailed methods may be left to individuals.

(d) Manage the available time effectively, including establishing and keeping to a rough timetable.

Further principles which emerge from study of such situations and are important for those steering to keep in mind are:

(a) If others are to contribute willingly and effectively they need to be able to understand and identify with the aims being pursued. This may mean regressing up a hierarchy or 'network' of more general aims to put the immediate situation in context.

(b) Silence or even 'yes I understand' does not necessarily imply either agreement or understanding. Observation of subsequent actions and listening for the relevance of subsequent contributions is necessary as a check.

(c) The more any individual has been able to contribute to the design of an outcome or way forward, the more committed he or she is likely to be to its achievement or implementation.

(d) The more people see their abilities, experience and ideas being respected and valued the more willing to help they tend to be. A steerer needs to listen carefully for the meaning, relevance and potential use of part or all of every contribution made by anyone joining and attempt to use or test it where practicable.

(e) Different ideas from different people may seem incompatible at first hearing yet combining elements of a number may both be possible and lead to a better result. In addition efforts by a steerer to get different ideas combined tends to encourage greater support, in the sense of building on each other's ideas, among the joiners (and therefore a move towards greater cooperation and teamwork).

(f) Steering effectively is a matter of balancing the need to get things done with getting the best out of each individual and with the encouragement of cooperation and teamwork among a group where several are involved. It requires observation of the whole 'wood', how people are thinking and feeling, how they are interacting, without losing sight of the 'trees', the job itself.

So far this chapter has concentrated on the part of the initiator of a job, the person who needs to steer or lead it. What of the joiners? If they have agreed to take part in some joint project or enterprise it would seem reasonable that there should be duties, responsibilities and therefore principles of behaviour for them to try to adopt. Certainly as the initiator, the person who sees the need to get something done, the steerer is initially at least 'in the driving seat', and may behave in ways which encourage more or less willingness on the part of the joiners to contribute to the success of the activity. Nevertheless, the mere fact of agreeing to take part points to some obligation for the joiners and requires an effort from them. While a steerer or leader may behave very skilfully to encourage cooperation, the choice to try to help or cooperate lies with the individual, and unless that choice is made efforts on the part of the steerer cannot wholly succeed.

It follows that many if not all of the principles that underlie effective steering also underlie effective joining, although their application will differ because of the difference in the respective situations. For example, any joiner who is trying to ensure that he or she contributes to the best of their ability to getting things done will need to:

(a) Ensure that he or she has a common understanding with the steerer and any other joiners of the situation and the aims to be pursued.
(b) Ensure that he or she understands the procedures to be followed and proposes modifications to these if judged helpful.
(c) Listen for the meaning, relevance and potential use of all or part of any other person's contributions and attempt to build on these to take matters forward.
(d) Frame and time his or her own contributions to ensure they are relevant both to what is being done and to the stage which has been reached.
(e) Observe and take steps to try to improve the way he or she is interacting with the others involved and how they are interacting with each other.

In general there is as much of an obligation on the part of a joiner to do whatever is necessary to get the job done well as there is on the part of a steerer. How often individuals are heard to comment after a meeting on the shortcomings of the chairman – no doubt if prompted the chairman could blame some of the members. A slight variation of the example on teachers and pupils quoted earlier seems appropriate. Everyone in a steering position might take as a maxim 'there are no bad joiners, only bad steerers', but every joiner 'there are no bad steerers, only bad joiners'. In other words everyone when steering or initiating an activity might take as an aim to make a success of those joining him or her, and everyone when joining to make a success of whoever is steering.

17

Leaders and followers

By this stage in a book describing the development of ideas concerned with managing and with getting things done it may seem surprising that 'leaders' and 'leadership' have received little mention. On early Coverdale courses 'leaders' were not appointed and groups were not encouraged to appoint 'leaders' or 'chairmen' for themselves merely on the grounds that 'groups usually have them'. This remained the position on Part 1 courses, although as the Part 2 course developed 'managers' (initially called 'duty officers') were appointed for periods of time. The way they 'managed' including how they gave a lead was then a topic for review and consideration. Nevertheless when in 1984 the Coverdale Organisation proposed and held a conference on leadership at York University, this led B.B.S. to comment that a striking feature of this venture was that leadership had indeed figured but little in Coverdale programmes.

He continued, 'This sudden appearance led me to ask the question – why was it that the topic of leadership had not played an important part in Coverdale programmes? One plausible answer seemed to be that what had been seen as important was that members of groups worked together to achieve agreed ends. In the Part 2 course the exercises called 'steering and joining' certainly distinguished the functions of those who come into a group at different times, some earlier than others; but no emphasis was laid on leadership as such. The question then must be asked when are leaders needed and what are they for?

'One useful answer is when a group needs someone to show or find the way, another may be where there is danger to be faced. Thus another reason for the lack of emphasis on leadership was that the timing of sessions on Part 1 courses did not allow matters of importance to be undertaken. Tasks were limited in scope; and it is not easy to imagine "leaders" emerging for such tasks as "produce four letter words" or "make a botanical display with material from the grounds of the hotel".'

The possibility of 'outward bound' type exercises may have been considered. These might have been seen as providing tasks of wider scope – and greater danger. To have adopted this (valuable) approach would have involved extensive changes in the design of courses, a design that had proved successful in highlighting valuable lessons relevant to working together to get things done. It could be argued that, given the short time available, the limited scope of the tasks used was both helpful and necessary in enabling course members to focus on those lessons. Certainly, as B.B.S. pointed out, 'The charge sometimes heard that Coverdale dealt in "trivial" tasks was countered by the fair comment that even such simple tasks revealed and drew attention to principles of great importance.'

If leaders are necessary when a group needs someone to find or show the way or where there is danger to be faced, 'what, if any, is the function of a follower or followers?

'In the discussion of steering and joining in the previous chapter, the point was made that joiners have useful contributions to make and these were outlined. In addition the functions of leaders have been discussed elsewhere – many books have been written about them. Much of this material concerns the relationship between leaders and followers. These are process issues and as usual I see them as treatable in two categories – personal inter-relations, in which charisma features prominently, and procedural matters. I deal here only with the latter.

'It is easy enough to say that the function of followers is to follow, but this does not make explicit that this is only possible where information about routes, methods and objectives is afforded clearly to followers by the leader.

'Even where a group of people operate in close proximity, it is important to ensure that all receive essential information, some of which will take the form of instructions. This is of course no new discovery, the history of sending messages and orders is a very long one.

'On a Coverdale course some years ago a group of managers exploring how to improve the communication of instructions pointed out that what needed to be conveyed and how it needed to be conveyed is affected by at least the factors of:

1 The state of knowledge or training of the recipient.
2 The urgency of the matter.
3 The degree of commitment of the recipient.

'Thus it was pointed out that the way a message was interpreted depended on the familiarity of the recipient with the task which was the content of the message. Another way of putting this is to say that the message must be adjusted to the state of readiness or training of the recipient. It is no use sending a message to prune the apple trees if the recipient has never pruned or does not know which trees are apples. The better trained the recipient the more concise can the instruction be.

'Again if the recipient is ready (i.e. familiar with the task), the more compact the message can be.' This is on the principle, clearly evident from the steering and joining work, that the more scope a recipient can be given to contribute in working out how to tackle a job the more committed he is likely to be to implementing the plans made.

'Complementary to the importance of instructions transmitted to members of a group is the need for messages to flow in the other direction, giving information about the state of the case or changes in it.

'As situations of any complexity develop it is not enough that such clear information is conveyed at the start, it will be needful that it is afforded as and when required by changes in the general situation. The only way in which the leader, or leaders, is in a position to know and to be able to pass this information back is when the followers keep the leader informed of any change that develops in the situation. However, in general, instructions will be conveyed from a single source while information about a situation may emanate from a number of sources, with the consequent risk of the leader's job being made difficult by the sheer amount of information. There may, therefore, be considerable skill in only transmitting important information to the centre. It seems that only training and experience will lead to the selection of that information.

'The importance of such a return flow of information cannot be overestimated. In times past, pictures of great battles show the forces deployed and the leader in such a position that he can see all that is going on.

'As operations increase in size and complexity so does the business of collecting and transmitting information in one direction and information and instructions in the other. It is easy to see that it soon becomes necessary to give practice and training in doing so to all concerned and not just the leaders.

'It is evident also that with the steady increase in the number and complexity of means of transmission the task of ensuring that important information is regularly supplied has not been simplified.'

18

Delegation

Delegation is generally taken to mean the entrusting of authority or power to someone else to act on one's behalf. As such it implies that the authority is temporary in that it may be taken back. The word also usually, but not necessarily, implies that the individual to whom a job is delegated will be carrying out whatever is necessary without the presence of, or detailed supervision and monitoring by, the person doing the delegating.

If one keeps these two points in mind virtually everything which has been said about steering can be said to apply to delegating and delegation as a particular class of steering and joining. The points made in Chapter 17 about the transmission of instructions in one direction and of information in the other are also relevant.

Thus preparing to delegate involves consideration of both the content of the situation to be tackled and how to make good use of the abilities of those to whom work is to be delegated. In considering the content, judgement must be made on the point in one's own thinking and dealing with the situation where one should start to communicate with the person receiving the job. The further one goes the less the opportunity for the latter to contribute his or her own facts, experience and ideas in determining what is to be done and how to do it. For example, let us suppose that communication starts at the point where the initiator is clear on what needs to be achieved in broad terms and the criteria to be met. In such an instance the person to whom authority is being delegated is able to contribute the relevant facts etc. he or she has towards defining what needs to be achieved more precisely, establishing what needs to be done and planning how to do it.

The factors to be taken into account in judging how far to go on the content of a situation before delegating are similar to those when preparing to steer i.e. the time available before there is an opportunity to communicate compared with that available afterwards; what is known of the skills, experience, knowledge, out-look, interests, of the person receiving the job and their likely willingness to help or level of commitment to the aims being pursued; the balance between ensuring as good an outcome as possible on a particular job and encouraging and developing will-ingness and ability on the part of the receiver to contribute on other jobs in the future. An important aspect of the way in which any manager assists the development of his subordinates is to be found in what and how he delegates to them. As Ralph Coverdale pointed out, the majority of managers in most organizations are promoted up out of jobs they have done very well. That makes them very proficient at the work of the level below them. As a result they often find it difficult to delegate without going further on the content of a situation than is necessary, thus limiting the scope for development of their subordinates.

Since, as we indicated at the beginning of this chapter, dele-gation usually implies allowing the receiver of a task to carry it out without the presence of the initiator, it makes it especially import-ant that both parties have a common understanding of:

(a) The situation.
(b) The aims to be pursued.
(c) The sort of outcome and quality required.
(d) Any other relevant thinking and work done already by the
     initiator and any information he or she sees as relevant.

Only if the briefing achieves this will the receiver of the job be able to proceed independently with the confidence that he or she is carrying out what is required. This is similar to any agent acting on behalf of a principal, where to negotiate successfully on the latter's behalf the former needs at the least to be clear on the aims and interests of the latter and on the criteria by which he or she will judge a satisfactory outcome.

Again as was pointed out in the section on transactions between steerers and joiners, there is a mutual obligation for the parties to make a success of the way the job is delegated. Just as the person delegating has a responsibility to provide an adequate briefing and whatever support is necessary, so the recipient has a responsibility for ensuring that he or she is briefed well and for seeking support if needed.

Much delegation within organizations takes place within an overall context where individuals are given authority to act and made accountable for their actions in connection with the position to which they have been appointed. Much of the normal day-to-day business of an organization proceeds with each individual doing his or her job without any overt 'delegation' from one person to another. However, situations frequently arise and time needs to be spent in getting things done which are not in the 'normal' day-to-day course of events. These may involve the need to delegate, either because the time is not available for an individual to deal with the situation alone, or different types of skill or expertise are required, or parts of the work fall within someone else's 'normal' area of authority and accountability, or where the initiator sees an opportunity to assist the development of a subordinate by giving him or her the opportunity to gain experience in tackling something which the manager might otherwise do himself or herself.

Similarly a job or function may be delegated to a junior or inexperienced person, if only to forestall the question, 'what will happen if X falls sick?', in order to educate them and give them the opportunity to learn. A variation of this can be seen to arise when a manager is away, thus providing an opportunity for the stand-in to show what he can do. In unfavourable and unfortunate settings such situations may be seen by a junior as opportunities to pass or supplant a senior. (Some years ago comment was made to the manager of a professional football club on the way in which club managers, when moving to another club, usually tried to take their assistant managers with them. He replied that the setting was such and the manager's job in most clubs was so insecure that he needed to be as sure as he possibly could that his assistant was not just waiting for the opportunity to take his job!)

19

Getting to yes – and getting to know

In 1981 the co-author of this book met Roger Fisher, Williston Professor of Law at Harvard and Director of the Harvard Negotiation Project. A UN official who had attended a Coverdale course run for the United Nations Development Programme effected the initial introduction on the grounds that it might be useful to compare notes. At an early meeting Roger Fisher handed over a pre-publication copy of *Getting To Yes – Negotiating Agreement Without Giving In* which he had written with Bill Ury. Subsequently some of the similarities and differences which had emerged at this first meeting between the work on negotiation going on at Harvard and our Coverdale work were discussed with B.B.S.

In commenting on the book he wrote, 'I still think it would be very valuable if there could be a companion volume *Getting To Know*. A certain amount of relevant matter is implicit in the chapter on dirty tricks.' And later, 'Is it worth distinguishing three cases?

1 Negotiations between principals.
2 Negotiations between principals, with a facilitator – honest broker or what you will.
3 Negotiations between agents (or ambassadors) representing principals.

'In 3, particularly, questions of credentials and powers become important...In all three situations, if you think of it, getting to know the people involved is crucial. Under examination my poor pun about "Yes" and "Know" reveals a very extensive range of conditions.'

The importance of people getting to know each other can be seen in the Coverdale work from the start, although it is equally true that little was done to explore the precise meaning of the phrase.

'People coming on courses found themselves in small groups with strangers (for the most part); they were encouraged to observe how people behaved and were encouraged to become a team, and they were assured that the performance of teams could far exceed the simple sum of individual performances. As the course proceeded they began to "get to know" each other. They tried to organize themselves, usually by appointing a chairman, and found that for teamwork it was important to know what each could do and how each could contribute.'

What is of very great significance is that this was being done against the background of people being invited to become a team and therefore it was assumed they would already have chosen to help each other, or would come to see the need to do so. This is clearly not the case where people have transactions with each other that involve negotiating – yet getting to know someone in order to be able to negotiate with them effectively (as distinct from work with them as part of a team) is equally important.

Some general points can be usefully made about how people do get to know each other.

When people meet for any reason they start to get to know or know about each other. Even where the interaction between them involves no more than chatting together, as for example the customers in the local public house, they form impressions and build up pictures of each other. How such impressions are formed and their effect on how people deal with each other are questions of importance to anyone trying to get things done where others are involved.

In the course of meeting and dealing with another person and of seeing him dealing with others one acquires through observation a succession of pieces of information. This observation of an individual is affected by the same conditions and seems to develop through the same stages as those described in Chapters 9 and 10 on observation. Thus the initial picture formed tends to grow in extent and comprehensiveness. A model of getting to know people may be illustrated in the following way. Draw in turn, as numbered, the lines shown in Figure 19.1 and as each is drawn look at what has been drawn and write down briefly what is there. Most people find that at certain stages they see some well-known shape developing, and succeeding lines confirm and support this; but there come stages when they are taken aback by the next addition, and find that the earlier pattern has to be replaced by a new one. (This

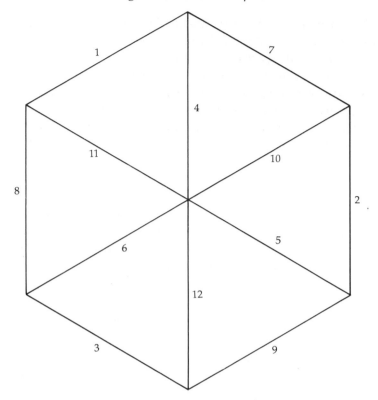

Figure 19.1

demonstration undoubtedly loses by being presented in this way, where the end state can be seen; even so, it may be worth going through the steps or trying it on someone who does not know the final appearance.)

The implication of this model is that most of us tend to get to know people as 'wholes', forming a picture quite quickly which is confirmed and supported by succeeding pieces of information, but which can change suddenly when a new piece does not seem to fit. Such a picture is enriched and often changed significantly by seeing a person in a different situation. For example, a professional footballer who, with his colleagues, attended a Coverdale course which involved tackling a number of small group exercises totally unrelated to football remarked that he had got to know them better in a few days than in two years' training and playing with them at the club.

The units of pieces of information which one acquires about

another person also tend to change in nature as one gets to know him or her over a longer period. As an example, if one studies a tennis player one might begin with strokes as a unit of information. This might soon be followed by increasingly longer units – rallies, games, sets, even matches, since on a professional circuit one may study a player in the number of matches he or she wins against other players. The information changes as the unit changes; someone may be a magnificent stroke player but little use in really hard-fought matches.

From such records different pictures may be drawn. Do we want to know, for example, what a person is like now or how he or she is developing? Neither, of course, will tell us for certain what they will be like when we meet next time. However, it is clear that the impressions we have formed already are relevant to the way in which we deal with someone the next time we meet. Similarly, if you have got to know them to some extent, then they will have got to know you and this will have a bearing on how they approach and deal with you. Thus before two people conduct any transaction with each other it is both possible and relevant for them to take stock of what they already know about each other:

(a) What has happened in previous meetings? What did the other party say or do? How did they behave?
(b) What do they like? What do they want? What are their aims, interests, concerns?
(c) What is their usual outlook? What timescale do they seem to think in?
(d) Do they tend to treat issues in an 'open' or 'closed' way?
(e) Are you likely to have dealings with each other in future?

The more that people get to know each other or about each other, the way they think and the way they act, the better able they are to make judgements on the extent to which they are prepared to trust each other. In practical terms this means, for example, how confident each is that the other will not try to mislead or deceive deliberately, take unfair advantage, use whatever is learnt from and about the other largely if not solely to personal ends, and that the other will keep his or her word, do whatever he or she says. In turn this influences how far each is willing to be open about the information they have and about their own aims, interests and concerns.

Where people have many dealings with each other, for example where they work together, it appears that they arrive through the normal course of events at what may be termed as working accommodations. They deal with each other in terms of the impressions they have formed. That does not mean necessarily that their transactions are efficient or lead to as good outcomes as they might wish. It may merely mean that they have reached a level which in normal circumstances they are willing to accept and do not wish to run the risk of upsetting. Going beyond that level, where it is necessary or desirable, may involve (a) more systematic efforts to get to know each other better and perhaps the opportunity to see each other in a different setting (as with the footballer quoted above) so that existing impressions/assumptions are challenged; (b) the choice by one or preferably both parties to try deliberately to improve the way they deal with each other.

20

Proceedings and transactions

At even a superficial level of consideration it is clear that people meet and have dealings with each other for a variety of reasons. A meeting purely for some social interaction differs from one to conduct an item of business and that differs again from one where people are working closely together to carry out a job of work.

In this last instance those involved are more likely to see themselves as colleagues or associates or as operating *within* some group or 'system' *with respect to those particular dealings*. In general terms these may usefully be described as 'proceedings', and it is easy to see that a major concern of all those involved should be, even if to an outsider often they do not appear to realize this, to ensure that those proceedings are as effective as possible. However, there are other dealings where the people involved see themselves as coming from different groups or systems in relation to the issue or matter in hand. They will see themselves as not only having differing interests but differing loyalties. Such dealings, which can be seen as crossing the boundary between two or more groups or systems, may reasonably be described as *transactions*.

As described in previous chapters, the Coverdale work really began by considering proceedings within a group, and this remains the starting point of the Coverdale basic experience or Part 1 course. However, inexorably over the years, as project work was undertaken in organizations and as courses were run for senior managers and directors (the early courses were developed for middle management), the work came to deal with transactions. There was no sharp transition and it is also fair to say that the significance of what was happening was not realized by those involved.

To illustrate how he had seen the aims of Coverdale work develop and widen and the consequent implications of this, B.B.S. outlined some major steps in that development. He started by referring to a Coverdale Part 2 course run with the Top Management Group of a company in 1966. (This was during the very first Coverdale project involving both the training of all levels of management and follow-through work on site.) The staff of the course wrote a report to which Ralph Coverdale attached his interpretations. In these he wrote, 'During Day 1 the group refer to "individual responsibilities", but there is no suggestion that all members of the group are responsible for the success of the group. Rather the phrasing and evidence suggest that members see themselves as responsible for their own functions. This is the exact reverse of the reality situation in a group and represents the philosophy behind a true rabble, each man seeking to impose his own decisions on the group in order to fulfil his own responsibilities.'

B.B.S. comments that rereading this some years later in 1982, 'I felt that Ralph Coverdale was expecting this particular Top Management Group to behave like a syndicate on a Part 1 course and was making no allowance for differences due to (a) their being senior managers (each with his own department), not middle management, and (b) their having worked together for two or more years. I felt that they had achieved what I suggested calling a "working accommodation" which might well differ from the state of a group described as having formed or jelled.

'In the earliest courses the state of "jelling" was aimed at, but in addition various qualities or activities were commended. Action was seen to be essential, so was taking responsibility for action. With these courage was commended, as also honesty and sincerity carrying with them aversion to role playing. Other matters of importance were aims and common comprehension of aims, proposing courses of action and supporting them, the identification of process skills and the turning of them to account.'

Ralph Coverdale's interpretation implied that he was taking an apparently simple view of the sort of group involved, i.e. one in which all members were deeply committed, where one would expect members to put the interests of that group before all else. In fact some of the comments of members of this Top Management Group reminded B.B.S. forcibly of Warren Bennis's comments on running an organization which is divided into large departments, that you may look for cooperation but not for teamwork. His point is that the responsibilities or 'loyalties' arising, where a man is in charge of a big department, make it impossible for him to be perfectly free and frank – to be committed to the welfare of the group with no strings attached.

However, even by this stage, in B.B.S.'s recollection, it had been acknowledged that what would help senior management would differ from what helped middle management, but what the difference was remained unclear. The descriptions he tried himself were completely inward-looking. Subsequently, courses for directors were in fact run but even by 1975 the concern remained primarily with the *proceedings* of groups and the value to participants was largely in relation to things they did within their own spheres of interest, whether group, department or organization.

Similarly, while by this time the Coverdale Organisation was deeply involved in work on organization development and in consultancy in addition to an extremely extensive programme of 'open' and in-house courses, Part 1 courses (especially 'open') were still concerned with the proceedings of a group while Part 2 involved interaction between departments but still primarily within an organization. In B.B.S.'s view the importance of interaction with the environment seemed not to have struck home and there was comparatively little about this issue in what followed. This was the case even for example during some internal seminars dealing with the making of policy at Board level and others on information processing, where one of the influences leading to these had been the recognition of the importance of information to the men at the top.

In passing B.B.S. noted, 'While the importance of good observation and the effective transmission of sound information cannot be overstated, it is unrealistic to suppose that in the real world one ever has all the information, and it is a matter of judgement for any individual whether more information is required and whether what could be obtained would repay the effort of obtaining it. Warren Bennis in his *The Unconscious Conspiracy* goes further and holds that there are great difficulties for a College President in obtaining true information about affairs within the College.'

In relation to information from the outside, 'strictly speaking one might say that obtaining information about one's environment is a kind of transaction, but if so it is a curious kind of transaction, because one of the parties may be totally unaware that information is being collected. This shows that collecting information may involve ethical issues not normally raised in transactions between two parties.'

In addition, in reviewing the work of Coverdale consultants with clients at the time, one thing stood out for B.B.S. The work leading up to a contract is different in kind from subsequent work as a consultant. The former, work leading to a contract, is a transaction between independent agencies; work subsequent to a contract can be seen as the proceedings of a group set up by the contract.

Finally, the introduction in 1981/82 to Professor Roger Fisher's work on negotiation at Harvard and the book *Getting to Yes*, and some subsequent collaboration in the development of a training course in negotiation, also raised the need to relate Coverdale work to negotiation, one very important form of transaction.

These developments, in the course of which Coverdale, which had actually begun by considering proceedings within a group, had come to deal with transactions, raised in B.B.S's view the crucial question, 'Can principles which were derived for and from the proceedings of a group, when this was conducted with the formation of a team in mind, be regarded as adequate for the operations of an organization?' This question leads to another, 'Can these principles be regarded as adequate for the transactions in which a person, persons or organization may become involved with others?'

The incident described at the start of this chapter concerning work with a particular Top Management Group during the first Coverdale project pointed one obvious important distinction between transactions and proceedings within a group as, for example, those considered in a Coverdale Part 1 course. The former involve loyalties far beyond anything envisaged in Coverdale Part 1 work or even Part 2. It is also clear that when Alex Smallwood wrote the article 'The Basic Philosophy of Coverdale Training' in 1976 (*Industrial and Commercial Training*, vol. 8 no. 1) loyalty was not even considered. Up to that time this was the most comprehensive attempt to set down in an article the principles of Coverdale training.

Reinforcing the point about the importance of loyalties in transactions B.B.S. drew attention to a letter to the *Daily Telegraph* (14 July 1982) by Andrew R. Cooper CBE, pointing out that it was, 'very relevant to the question we have acknowledged, namely loyalties.'

The writer had been Member for Personnel on the Central Electricity Generating Board. 'I have written to him agreeing, but saying that I have discovered no simple way of putting priorities in order.'

Cooper's letter made the point forcibly to those union leaders who were appealing to their members to remember where their loyalties lay that there were many loyalties to be remembered by any individual member. These included that to his neighbour, to the man who pays his wages (not his employer but his customer), to his family, to his country, to his religion, to himself in the sense of what sort of man he thought he was and wished to be remembered as. It concluded that truly all men should think of their loyalties, but they should get their priorities right.

The need to weigh differing loyalties is one factor that makes transactions and proceedings different in their demands on people. Another difference lies in aims. While noting that there are many points in common between cooperation and negotiation, B.B.S. observed, 'I find J. G. Cross in *The Economics of Bargaining* saying (in his chapter on the use of dirty tricks), "Such devices are too likely to be interpreted as evidence of bad faith, and the objective of the bargaining process is, after all, cooperation." Remarks such as this (which I don't accept) make me more inclined to begin with transactions and classify them after use and study, rather than to pick out what appears to be an important variety (negotiation) to begin with.

'A good deal of the negotiation literature seems to be concerned with mathematical approaches to bargaining. I have not found these very illuminating; they are concerned with possibilities, but not, so far as I can see, with aims and policies. Coddington (in *Theories of the Bargaining Process*) lists and describes seven mathematical approaches, but the two quotations that follow show that the ends are open:

1 "It seems likely that all conflict situations in reality have some inner dynamics which can only be accepted, but at the same time leave some room for active choice." (page 79)
2 "At the theoretical level the long-term aspects of bargaining processes are completely unexplored." (page 80)

'It would simplify matters greatly if one could find evidence of some general principle, perhaps one to which one could turn when all others failed. But I don't think the evidence points that way. Coddington quotes from Siegel and Fouraker's *Bargaining and Group Decision Making*, "The basic structure of the situation has the essential characteristic of many social conflict situations. In one sense, a situation of bilateral monopoly appeals to the mutual interests of the participants and would seem to call for harmonious cooperation between them. In another, the interests of the participants are exactly in opposition and acrimonious competition would seem to be the behaviour norm. Social scientists are particularly concerned with systems of decision-making whereby such conflicts are resolved."

'The existence of such an opposition is neatly expressed in Leonard Woolley's *Dead Towns and Living Men* when talking of the Kurds, "(there is, by the way, no such thing as dishonesty when enemies deal together, though you should not cheat a friend)."

'Overall I cannot agree that the situation of bargaining is conformable to the situation of team-building. One of the authors I have consulted points out that in the course of bargaining one gets to know the other side better. This is an important feature of the situation but it does not mean either that your aims become the same or that you come to like each other better. It is a serious matter if in bargaining you allow either liking or disliking for the other to affect your judgement. This is surely one of the reasons why important negotiations are usually conducted by agents. If the agent's actions are affected by likes or dislikes this is liable to affect the trust between agent and principal. But it is important to recognize that when agents are introduced so is the question of loyalty.

'It occurred to me that, since no distinction had been drawn between the proceedings and the transactions of a group until recently, the principles enunciated in Alex Smallwood's article might cover both in some cases. Rereading the article leaves me convinced that what is in it is primarily, if not exclusively, concerned with proceedings. If I am right this means that a search for principles applicable to transactions should go on.

'I cannot pretend to have cleared matters up entirely but I have come across some distinctions that I find useful and can suggest one or two principles which may be helpful. The position as I see it now is set out below. A lot of it is tentative and unfinished.

'*Proceedings* are typically activities such as take place within a Coverdale Part 1 team or similar group. The group deals with a task by applying a systematic approach to getting things done. Within such a group one aspect is that the individuals have made the *choice to help*, although how to help in the circumstances of the case may have to be learnt. Developments to be expected within the group are a progressive getting to know each other, acting in terms of others in the group as known, towards, finally, collective responsibility (as in Cabinet?).

'*Transactions* are activities involving independent individuals or groups. Simple transactions can be matters of exchange (purchase) or gift and can include ideas as well as goods or chattels. The basic object of a transaction is that both sides are, as a result, better off and willing to do business again. When these conditions are fulfilled we may talk of a satisfactory transaction. Some principles that arise, if the conditions are to be fulfilled, are *do as you would be done by* and *fairness*. Not all transactions are satisfactory and in such instances one party may be able to force the other to accept or comply. Changes taking place over a period of time with repeated transactions are that the parties get to know each other better, with the possibility that this may lead to the building of mutual confidence and trust.

'*Negotiation* is a form of transaction where one or both parties aim to improve their state or the terms of an exchange. It is often found that much time is required to find conditions that are acceptable to both sides. Not infrequently negotiations are conducted through agents. When agents are involved one also finds questions of loyalty arising.

'If my attempted analysis of proceedings and transactions is at all valid I think it shows that the latter, including negotiations, differ in quite important ways. Something else that stands out is the importance of getting to know. It would be of great value to discover whether this is a natural process which may be peculiar to the circumstances of any case or whether one can discover methods or principles which make the results more readily accessible or more useful. Thus, for example, one might in the process of getting to know someone learn that they are dedicated collectors of stamps or dog fanciers, but whether this would help in buying a house from them is not clear. This leads immediately to the question what would you want to know in such situations? Can we devise a series of questions, to be answered by word of mouth or by observation, to enable us to build ideas into pictures or portraits of people we meet?'

A further point that stands out is that any principle suggested for transactions, e.g. 'do as you would be done by' (which seems to apply in all or virtually all circumstances), good manners, firmness and sticking to arrangements made, ought to be included in any list for proceedings, almost as a matter of course. However, those for transactions must cover a wider range of circumstances including those where the question of loyalties is very important and where people have yet to get to know each other. It would appear that many of the principles will be the same but their relative import-ance will differ.

Some support for this view can be found in comparing the Coverdale approach (to proceedings) to an approach to mediation as set out in *International Mediation: A Working Guide* by Roger Fisher. As B.B.S. commented, 'It is of interest that the book is divided into parts: (a) the human problem; (b) the inventing prob-lem; and (c) the procedural problem.

'If I reworded these as: (a) process or human interaction; (b) what has to be done; (c) process or procedure; there is suggested an interesting link to the Coverdale approach. There isn't an exact equivalence and the differences are worth examining. As I recall it one Coverdale presentation was to speak of:

1 Task
2 Process

'I was keen that 2 should be divided into (a) procedure and (b) human interaction and I suggested that in practice one would tackle a situation in that order. (*Note*: I am fairly sure now that a group cannot reasonably be expected to treat a task competently until they have worked out a procedure for themselves.) Speaking in terms of the proceedings of a group or team, this meant agreeing procedures before tackling human interaction, on the grounds that human interaction was less likely to cause trouble if procedures had been agreed. The big difference is, I suggest, that in the Coverdale Part 1 case one assumed that one was dealing with a group in which choice to help had been made, and it now looks to me as if one assumed also that the members had got to know one another.

'In the negotiating situation these assumptions cannot be made, and so it seems to me that the first steps to be taken are those which lead to *getting to know* and are concerned with process in the sense of human interaction' (rather than with procedures). 'Then the end product of negotiation could be something like a Coverdale Part 1 Team' (in that people who had learnt to negotiate together effec-tively over a period of time should have got to know each other and might have concluded that they needed in a sense to help each other resolve issues and conduct their negotiations both efficiently and amicably) 'but it also becomes clear that the early stages of transactions and negotiations cannot be treated with the same methods as Coverdale Part 1 groups. Once again proceedings and transactions can be seen to differ.'

Later still, after some further exchanges between us, B.B.S. wrote, 'When we talked about the principles underlying Coverdale work, e.g. as set out in Alex Smallwood's article, I raised again the question as to whether principles worked out for Coverdale Part 1 teams would still hold for larger groups. Your answer was that probably in the minds of Coverdale workers these principles had been assumed, used, and applied in progressively larger groups, without overt consideration.

'I think this may well be the case but such a growth may be insidious and in the end may make operators vulnerable. If we look back at what was basic in relation to Part 1 teams don't we find a need for agreement as to aim and a basic *choice to help* and others. As groups grow in size it almost certainly becomes less safe to make these assumptions. There may well be some others to which the same argument would apply. I suggest it would be useful to take the list of principles in Alex Smallwood's article and consider how valid each remains as the size and nature of the group concerned grows. I would go further and offer as a practical observation that, if one is involved with a group of say 30 to 50, it is unrealistic to think that one can obtain conclusions or opinions that represent the views of the group in less than two days. Hence the emphasis on getting to know. What assumptions can you make before you get to know?

'Anselm Strauss (*Negotiations: Varieties, Contexts, Processes and Social Order*) describes negotiation as a means to getting things accomplished. To what extent could we say, on that basis, that the procedures of negotiation should follow the steps of "a systematic approach to getting things done"? Here again we meet the question of community of aims. Unless community of aims exists *at some level* it is not possible to embark on "a systematic approach".

'On this basis arms reduction by the great powers, the Falkland Islands, and many wage disputes would be unnegotiable – so one may need to consider the preparatory stages which lead to a situation where aims are agreed, and then negotiation of procedures and resources becomes possible. It may be a quibble to say that such a phase is not negotiation, but preparatory to it – but as there are situations, e.g. Geneva talks, where the participants take years before some aims can be agreed, clearly this is an important phase, and the question now becomes, what principles apply in this preparatory phase? Is this a phase before the participants have got to know each other, before mutual trust and confidence has been built or has grown? If so what is the climate, what are the principles operating? Is this a region where Voltaire's saying applies, that speech was given to us to conceal our thoughts?

'Are there, for instance, stages at which:

1 One seeks to obtain maximum advantage.
2 One gets to know the other side and then aims to achieve a fair compromise.
3 One aims to become a team and for the team to find a joint way forward?'

Howard Raiffa, in his book *The Art and Science of Negotiating*, suggests that the behaviour and way of operating that people adopt and expect from each other may be regarded as falling on a continuum. At one end people are highly cooperative; at the other (where one party sees the other as threatening seriously aims and values which he holds) violently antagonistic. Using Raiffa's terms, at one end we have 'strident antagonists', at the other 'fully cooperative partners', but in the middle, where most people would tend to see themselves in most of their negotiations, we have 'cooperative antagonists'. By this is meant that they:

(a) Recognize they have differences of interests; would like to find a mutually acceptable way forward but expect all parties to be primarily worried about their own interests.
(b) Do not have malevolent intentions, nor are they altruistically inclined.
(c) Are slightly distrustful of one another; each expects the other to try to make out a good case for his own side and to indulge in 'strategic posturing'.
(d) Are not confident that the others will be truthful but would like to be truthful themselves.
(e) Expect power will be used gracefully, that all parties will abide by the law, and that all joint agreements will be honoured.

In considering this, B.B.S. commented, 'I have distinct reservations about putting strident antagonists and fully cooperative partners at opposite ends of a scale. They don't sound to me as if they are simple opposites but I have difficulty in seeing better terms. John Wellens (in the journal *Industrial and Commercial Training*) made much use of the term "adversarial" in his articles (particularly in relation to the defects he saw in trade unionism). Using this concept I find that some points become clearer, though one still lacks a simple term at the other end such as "partner", but preferably one which conveys the sense of "helping of choice". If employers and union members find themselves in the same body there can be an underlying adversarial tone yet results may be obtained. Could one then talk of collaboration rather than cooperation? Or can you see a better word? At the other end of the scale one can see both sides partaking in a contest (or match) which does not have the adversarial tones of a conflict.

'Turning back to negotiation, one can distinguish the case where the two (two for simplicity) sides have different interests but are concerned to achieve a result which is good or acceptable on both sides, from the case where both sides are out to do the other down (or to get the best for oneself). Does one need to consider a third case where the aims of the two sides differ, one being out for itself and the other to get the best for both?

'I fear that this approach brings me back to the starting point. What are the principles of action which you could recommend in transactions – or are you going to say to people "your principles are no concern of mine, here are a number of gambits you can use"?

'It is not irrelevant that when I turned to Raiffa's book beginning, as usual, with the last chapter, I found that was where ethical issues were treated.'

Later still B.B.S. wrote, 'In recent letters I have been suggesting that one should seek a basis of principles for transactions. I thought Raiffa's book offered such a list. In today's *Daily Telegraph* is a short article by O'Sullivan from Harvard. In this he raises some unanswered questions about the Harvard Negotiation Project approach as it stands. I take some comfort from this, but it looks as if my suggestion needs to be extended. Not only do we need principles on which the various people involved in transactions would act, we need more. I used to quote the ambassador, who said that when he sat down at the negotiating table with people, what he first determined was what were their powers and what were their credentials. Now I should say we need that and more, we need to know their aims and their principles of action.

'All of which brings back what I said when first thinking about

Fisher and his work. We need "getting to know" to complement "getting to yes".

'Thus if people are to be helped to derive from experience principles to guide their behaviour in transactions (including negotiations) what begins to look needful then is to start a group of people with an initial situation of "free for all" or "no holds barred". People then need to be helped to form impressions of one another and thence derive rules to allow transactions to take place.

'It has been said that first impressions are most important and that they are formed almost instantaneously. But we also know that first impressions can be belied. How much time and interaction would be needed to allow the eduction of rules to cover transactions? Could this be done in a reasonable time to allow practical courses to be set up?

'My personal opinion is that there will be no absolute answer to this question; that one can build reliable impressions of others most of the time, but that there will always remain cases or a proportion of cases where first impressions, or even what seem well-founded impressions, are no longer borne out. It looks to me as if one effect of such an approach would be to produce different sets of rules or principles from different groups, though we might find particular rules cropping up frequently.

'I think one prerequisite would be to compile a list of topics or questions on which one could seek information. Thus what does X like?, What does X want?, What are X's aims? and so on. But if one goes this way one will need to devise methods or approaches which would elicit the answers.

'Another question one would need to answer would be could you expect people to cooperate in answering and in providing the information you seek or would you have to reach answers by inference from behaviour?'

From the consideration of proceedings, transactions and negotiation above some key points seem clear:

1 The effective conduct of proceedings and the effective conduct of transactions (including negotiations) differ in their demands on people.
2 Principles which can be advanced as guides to action when conducting transactions need to cover a wider range of circumstances than those for conducting proceedings.

3 Principles for transactions need to take much more account of the fact that:
   (a) Those involved will have loyalties and responsibilities to others beyond the immediate group i.e. those with whom they are dealing.
   (b) The parties may not have got to know each other.
   (c) One or more of the parties involved may be out to extract the maximum advantage rather than to achieve an acceptable compromise or (as should be the case with proceedings) to find a joint way forward.
4 Where people do see themselves as part of a group in respect to a situation and choose to help each other in tackling it, the logical order for doing so is:
   (a) Work out some procedures for doing so.
   (b) Tackle the substance or content of the situation ('task') by establishing community of aims *at some level* and applying a systematic approach.
   (c) Tackle any human interaction issues that arise in the course of doing so. Obviously in the course of this they will continue to get to know each other better.
5 Where, perhaps because of other loyalties or because they have not yet got to know each other, they do not see themselves as part of a group in respect to the particular situation, the logical order seems to be different:
   (a) To tackle human interaction in the sense of discovering more about each other (including each other's aims, principles of action, powers and credentials).
   (b) To establish some procedures to help deal with the situation.
   (c) To tackle the substance or content ('task').
6 Thus in transactions (including in particular negotiations) what is important initially is methods/ways for the parties to get to know each other. From this may or may not develop a willingness for the parties to collaborate in arriving at an acceptable outcome in the particular situation – and hence a need to establish procedures for doing so.
7 A training course to help people derive principles for guiding their behaviour in transactions needs to start at a different point from one concerned with proceedings.

21

Individual and team development

From very early in the development of Coverdale Training there was heavy emphasis on the benefits of teamwork. Indeed during the latter part of the 1960s the courses were entitled 'The Practice of Teamwork'. However, in the early 1970s teamwork as a concept seemed to be less popular. For example, the head of the staff college of a major British industry told Ralph Coverdale that what industry was really looking for – and what he saw Coverdale Training as providing – was individual manager development. Seeing the great marketing opportunities for training aimed primarily at helping managers to personal development, Coverdale caused a change of direction, emphasizing that on the course the group was 'a vehicle to enable the individual to learn'. In line with this the title of the courses changed to 'The Practice of Management Principles' – a title which had also been used on the courses run earlier by Coverdale when he was at Esso Petroleum.

The difference is between a course directed to helping participants to personal development in the belief that such individuals will produce better teams (and ultimately organizations), on the one hand, and, on the other, a course which puts teamwork first. In the latter, participants are helped to discover the resources which others (and they themselves) bring with them and to enable all the available resources to be brought into operation in the work of the team. Participants are thus explicitly invited to help others as well as themselves, and it is believed that understanding and achieving this brings personal development at the same time. Making personal development preeminent, as happened for a period in the 1970s, led to the temporary loss of what had been an important feature of Coverdale Training, namely the value of making this conscious 'choice to help' and the implications of doing so.

At the end of the 1970s some of those involved in running Coverdale courses expressed concern at the effects of the diminishing emphasis on teamwork, and there was a swing away from the movement to make personal development the main aim. However, others took a different view and it seemed clear that the matter would remain contentious and surface from time to time. Therefore in 1983 B.B.S. wrote on the following lines with a proposal to try to deal with the issue.

'As when this matter came up before, I feel that any proposal to make personal development the prime objective of courses would mean abandoning the most characteristic feature of Coverdale work, namely the value of the "choice to help" and the resultant emphasis on cooperation and teamwork.

'Your introduction to R. Fisher and (the work on) negotiation make it important to rethink the structure of courses and the lessons likely to be drawn. I think it can be done so that the whole hangs together.

'What I have done so far is to list the topics which need to be introduced, setting them out roughly in order of complexity. Generally speaking then, they might be introduced in that order.

1 When individuals set to work, they can be helped to work systematically.
2 When a number of individuals meet, they need to get to know one another.
3 If an individual tackles a job: (a) it helps to distinguish preparation, action and review, and to learn by applying those concepts; (b) it helps to be clear about aims.
4 If more than one individual is present, they can help each other by watching. They can begin to know each other better by exchanging observations and descriptions of experience. These exchanges also help learning.
5 Simple transactions may be seen as jobs involving more than one person. What are the aims? What principles of action emerge?
6 Transactions where one or more of the persons involved tries to secure an improvement in terms. Negotiation is entailed. What principles emerge?
7 Jobs requiring more than one person: (a) effects of the choice to

help; (b) cooperation; (c) allocation of function in relation to skill; (d) mutual support.

8 Jobs requiring more than one person where one or more have the opportunity or necessity to do some work in advance of others joining them. Further issues arise, some to "steering" and some to "joining".

9 Development of teams – agreement on aims, agreement on procedures, use of process skills and of technical skills; the proceedings of groups.

10 Organizing and being organized.

'Obviously I haven't put in all the features at each stage. My feeling is that, if anyone went through such a course, they could say they had developed personally and with respect to cooperation.

'What would make me uneasy would be if someone could make a start on such a series of exercises as I have suggested and say after a while, "Now I understand how to conduct my business competently, I don't need any more, certainly not any of that stuff about getting on with people."

'In spite of this risk, it seems to me that there is a certain rightness about beginning with individuals and how they conduct affairs and how they get to know others, leading to transactions with others (some of these could involve negotiation). Surely it is from this situation that others arise where jobs are too big or too time consuming and so people have to work together. From this situation one can move naturally to others where what is at issue is how to organize numbers of people working together (and so to the study of the proceedings of groups), which would pick up with the situation of a Coverdale Part 1 course as it is now.

'If such an approach were to be attempted, there would be immediately a need to review and revise the situations and groupings on courses. A lot of preliminary work would be needed. I suggest that a course (or series of courses) of such a kind would help people to work better individually and in groups (it would not be needful to contrast individual development with teamwork).'

Later in the same letter he observed, 'One thing which this approach has brought out in addition is that teamwork was not what the Coverdale course originally set out to achieve. Ralph Coverdale wanted managers who could manage people (as well as being good at steelmaking) and he was impressed by the power of a group. The idea of groups "forming" turned out to be doubtfully attainable and doubtfully useful. It was replaced by something which appeared attainable and useful. At this stage groups were encouraged to try to work together as a team.

'Since none of the groups on courses were going to stay together, it had to be the experience of forming a team which was at issue and could be held to be of value.

'I think much subsequent work shows that teamwork is a poor ultimate aim. (It is in my terminology a good example of indirection and may be what is sometimes called sub-optimization. In other words teamwork is only part of the story.) Would it help to give as an aim "working well on jobs with others"?'

To the best of the authors' knowledge at the time of writing the structure of Coverdale open courses remains broadly the same as when this was written. This structure is well-established, of proven value and successful; it is also recognized as such by organizations sending their staff to attend the courses. A radical restructuring on the lines proposed would seem to change the whole nature of the courses being offered and therefore be difficult to carry out. It might also be argued that therefore it was no longer 'Coverdale Training' as it would be recognized by the great majority of people.

They are familiar with a Part 1 course where participants started and remained for most of a week in the same small group, focusing on getting that group to work together as a team in getting things done, with an aim beyond this that individuals should identify from that experience 'lessons' for use in their differing situations after the course. They would probably also know that the Part 2 course, attended by a significant proportion of people a short period after their Part 1, was designed to give the experience of applying those lessons in a variety of different groups and differing situations. (It had originally been designed in fact to meet the point made by managers that, while the experience of team formation was valuable, there were in practice not many permanent teams in industry and business. What did happen was that they found themselves attending a working party on something, then moving off to a meeting with different people on something else, then discussing a third issue with others, and so on. They thus had the need to help get 'new' groups under way quickly, get useful work done and then break up without the apparent 'luxury' of being able to form permanent teams.)

However, if one were starting afresh the restructuring proposed seems more logical and potentially more efficient. Some courses have been developed and run based broadly on the structure suggested. From that experience there is little doubt that such a structure does enable participants to build up a coherent and logical picture of what is involved in getting things done as they meet situations of greater complexity in terms of the involvement of and interactions with others. It does not confuse the power of the small group as a learning method with the importance of teamwork as one aspect of working well with others. Finally, and crucially, it still retains the value of 'the choice to help'. For as B.B.S. has written elsewhere, 'In working out a joint enterprise it is important to become alive to process issues, but this in itself is not enough for effectiveness. Confidence, commitment, involvement and participation are all wanted. None of them will come about unless men choose to help each other.'

22

Development of teams

Much has been written about the value of teamwork and the desirability of developing teams. However, many things are necessary to enable people to get things done reasonably effectively before the development of teams per se becomes an important factor. It seems that too readily the assumption may be made that teams are a panacea for all difficulties of management. Such an assumption arises from treating teams as ends in themselves rather than as very useful means or tools for getting things done in certain circumstances.

What are some of those circumstances? We have already considered in Chapter 21 how the situation develops and additional concepts and principles arise as we move from doing things alone to needing to involve others in simple transactions, to a point where we actually require others to get something done. At what point does it become useful to think in terms of developing teams? Obviously encouraging teamwork, in the sense of effective cooperation among those involved is helpful as soon as coordination of any sort is necessary. Thus anyone participating whether as steerer or as joiner in the type of situation described in Chapter 16 on steering and joining will assist the performance of the group by applying the ideas and principles noted there. These can be seen as very important elements of what we mean by teamwork. Similarly any body of people where the members see themselves as operating within one group or system will need to apply these same principles in seeking a satisfactory level of performance. However, deliberately building or developing permanent or semi-permanent teams (i.e. teams which will last for a significant period of time and over a number of projects) seems to imply rather more than developing teamwork for the purposes of getting a specific job or jobs done well. When might it be desirable to go further and think in terms of developing teams?

Several circumstances come to mind. An essential feature of good teamwork is that the members of a group know enough about each other for the contribution of each to be such as to employ the skill and characteristics of all to the best advantage. Acquiring this knowledge is not easy, particularly for example in the circumstances which obtain within most business organizations, where the normal day-to-day working contacts are confined largely to exchanging information. Where groups do take time to review the way they work together and plan to improve that process the individuals gain a wider knowledge of each other. It is common on Coverdale training courses for groups to engage enthusiastically in process planning aimed at improving their operation and then, within a matter of hours, neglect the plans made. One reasonable explanation is that the individuals have got to know each other well enough to adjust their own personal behaviour to take account of each other's characteristics. Thus the effort that went into the process planning has not been lost. For the process of establishing agreement on procedures has made work easier and, in addition, the procedures are there to be revived if occasion demands. Perhaps this is something close to what is often called the Hawthorne effect. If so, its importance is that it suggests that in a situation where teamwork may not be strictly necessary, teams may be better able than individuals to resist stress. Similarly, team formation may be useful in lessening anxiety or fear. As Lewis Carroll wrote of the Beaver and the Butcher Boy:

> 'But the valley grew narrower and narrower still,
>   And the evening got darker and colder,
> Till (merely from nervousness, not from goodwill)
>   They marched along shoulder to shoulder.'

We have referred earlier to 'closed' and 'open' situations, and shown how it is possible to 'close down' and limit the scope of a job by focusing on limited aims or to 'open it up' and explore wider possibilities. Treating situations as open requires confidence. Precise outcomes cannot be determined in advance and a high tolerance for ambiguity and willingness to venture into the unknown is needed. Therefore, it can be disturbing for an individual or a group to face an open situation. Where the members of a group have learned to work together well they are likely to be able better to resist the stress resulting from having to tackle open situations. As a result they are more likely to open situations up than groups which have not learned to work well together. There is thus a clear relationship between level of performance and teamwork, since for a group to achieve a high level necessitates it being able to make effective use of all the skills of members, the task or professional skills and knowledge and the thinking and interpersonal skills. Therefore, a high degree of teamwork is needed in the interaction between the members.

Clearly there *are* good reasons for developing teams or engaging in deliberate efforts at team-building as a means of encouraging teamwork where that is necessary to get things done at the level of performance desired. However, it is how people who work together treat a particular situation and how they formulate the aims to be pursued in tackling it that determine whether the situation calls for teamwork or not. Here we encounter almost a 'chicken and egg' situation. Groups of individuals which, while focusing on achieving high-quality results in getting things done, have developed a high degree of teamwork in their operation are more likely to formulate aims where teamwork is required. Nevertheless, both in developing teams and in encouraging teamwork, it is essential that the focus remains firmly on getting things done, so that teams are not developed as ends in themselves.

Given that good reasons for developing teams exist, how does one go about it? The most important clue lies in what has been emphasized above. Since the way in which people interact is an important factor affecting a team's effectiveness, it appears logical to invite those who interact regularly (e.g. management 'teams') to study their processes of interaction with a view to improving them. However, it has long been clear that groups concerned solely with interpersonal relations tend to become 'cosy' groups, delightful to belong to but ineffective since they are not concerned with any job. It is true that any team-building exercise is likely to leave the members of the team excited and stimulated by the experience. This is a feature of almost all forms of group work and group training. (As B.B.S. noted, after talking with someone who had attended a T-group and reported feelings of euphoria, of getting to know splendid people and of being able to cope with anything, it is clear that feeling is not enough: you must do things. The points listed above suggested to me that the effects of a small group course would be much the same whatever the theoretical background underlying it. One should not, therefore, be surprised if someone comes away saying it was wonderful: the fact that the experience was wonderful does not mean necessarily that the principles can be applied elsewhere.) The enthusiasm generated by a team-building exercise is unlikely to last unless improvement in task achievement is achieved. A group of individuals does not become a team solely by reason of the interpersonal relations. An essential ingredient of teamwork for any group, whether a management 'group' or a football 'team' is that the 'task' skills, as well as the interpersonal skills, of each member should be applied appropriately. In addition the interpersonal relationships that arise within a group need not be the same for different tasks, since the pattern of task skills, in kind or order of application, will differ from task to task i.e. contribution will be needed from different individuals in different combinations at different times.

The implications of the above for developing teams are:

1 Teamwork needs to be seen not as an end in itself but as a very valuable means for tackling situations and getting things done.
2 The focus in reviewing and planning to improve performance must be on learning to use both the task skills and knowledge and the interpersonal skills available within the group *in order to get things done.*
3 Teams developed with these points in mind will either close situations down or open situations up as necessary to achieve high level task results.

Developing such teams involves encouraging them to review *and* plan to improve their performance. Such a review requires consideration to be given to what is being done (how far the aims and success criteria are being met), how the resources, both physical and human, are being used, the methods and procedures being applied, as well as how people are interacting. While some of the information for such a review comes from the results achieved, other relevant information comes from the observations of the individuals involved. As pointed out in Chapter 9 on observation, there are a number of stages through which the ability to make useful observations tends to develop. Groups of individuals aiming to become teams, or merely aiming to improve their teamwork, need not only to exchange observations of what has happened and how it has happened (both what has gone well and what badly). They need to share their interpretations of likely causes of these successes and difficulties and to establish what needs to be done to extend the causes of success and to overcome those of difficulty. Their proposals may take the form of procedures, 'rules of thumb' or practices to be followed and, where relevant, they may need to be supported by more detailed plans to ensure they are followed when the occasion demands.

Some further points about reviewing and planning to improve group performance are relevant. First, the situation is always more usefully regarded as 'open', in that one can never have all the information necessary to define a clear solution. One will therefore always be working on part of the information, interpretations put forward as underlying causes of success and difficulty will only be possible explanations and proposals based on them will need to be tested, reviewed and probably modified in the light of experience if the desired improvement is to be achieved. An appropriate model is like the one described in Chapter 5 on the Turbine Theory of Action.

Second, a sound balance needs to be maintained between the consideration of successes and difficulties. Most groups, like most individuals, soon lose confidence if attention is given only to failure. Groups which focus solely on successes may well become complacent. Moreover, it is inefficient to ignore one or the other since interpretations and ideas for improvement may stem from either and from comparing and contrasting the two.

Third, there is a good case for saying that in reviewing performance priority should be given to procedural matters, which are essentially questions of agreement and self-discipline within a group. For if these are dealt with personal and interpersonal difficulties will diminish and any such difficulties remaining can be tackled against the background of improvement and progress already made.

Finally, any group is of course an 'open' system in that it has transactions with its environment. If its focus strays from getting things done and it becomes what has been described earlier as a 'cosy group', then the members may insulate themselves from outside information and operate on assumptions which such information might cause them to question. A striking example of this can be seen in the working of the group which advised US President Kennedy on the Bay of Pigs invasion of Cuba (as described in *Victims of Groupthink* by Irving L. Janis). The President and his key advisers are said to have approved the invasion plan on the basis of a number of assumptions, each of which was wrong. Even when they first began to discuss the plan sufficient evidence was available to indicate that their assumptions were much too shaky. They could have obtained and used the crucial information beforehand to correct their false assumptions if at the group meetings they had been more critical and probing in fulfilling their advisory roles.

23

Systems and systems thinking

From the early 1960s Ralph Coverdale presented on courses his ideas about kinds of systems. He distinguished four systems:

1 *Static*	e.g. the exact historical systems of accountancy.
2 *Mechanistic*	e.g. the dynamic and mechanical or technical systems of technology.
3 *Organic*	e.g. the living systems of plants and animals
4 *Ethical*	e.g. man with his ability to hold ethical values.

These were built on the distinction made by Burns and Stalker in *The Management of Innovation* between mechanistic and organic organizations.

With the expansion of Coverdale work to increasingly broader fields came a growth of interest in organizations and 'systems thinking'. One particular stimulus among others was to look at the ideas of Professor Kenneth Boulding in this latter field. This came with the remark of a participant on a course that it was all very well to talk of the four systems but 'what about the other five?' An outcome of this particular reference to Boulding's work and of the general interest in systems and systems thinking was an internal seminar run by B.B.S. on this topic.

At this he set out some areas of interest for Coverdale staff:

1 *A systematic approach* – in this phrase, when it was coined, systematic was adopted as a near-synonym for orderly.
2 *A system* – in general this means a collection of objects, people, ideas or concepts. The *Concise Oxford Dictionary* definition is a complex whole, set of connected things or parts, organized body of material or immaterial things. Von Bertalanffy talks of a complex

of interacting elements, Ross Ashby of any set of variables selected from those available. The underlying idea, from its derivation from the Greek, is one of standing together and being inter-related. In a systems approach one deals with wholes: this leads to methods and outlook appropriate to wholes rather than to analytical methods.

3 *A closed system* lies within a boundary. Strictly speaking nothing crosses the boundary so that if the contents are fully specified anything that can happen is determined.

4 *An open system* has a boundary that is either permeable or has gaps. Thus there can be inflow or intake from the environment and there can be output or outflow to the environment.

It has been argued that in the past management and organizations have been regarded and treated as if closed systems and that for the future it is important to regard them as open systems.

Moving on to considering Ralph Coverdale's ideas about kinds of systems he pointed out that both these and the ideas of Burns and Stalker could be seen as aspects of general systems theory, a useful presentation of which was to be found in an article with that title by Boulding (*Management Science* vol. 2, no. 3, April 1956), from which the following can be derived:

Static structure	The level of *frameworks*. The geography and anatomy of the universe. 'Stuff' and its properties.
Simple dynamic systems	The level of *clockworks*. Systems with pre-determined necessary motions. Energy and control lie *outside*.
Control mechanisms/cybernetic systems	The level of the *thermostat*. The transmission and interpretation of information is an essential part of the system. The homeostatic model, designed to maintain states within closed systems and of great importance in physiology, is an example of a cybernetic mechanism. At this level the principle of feedback arises.
Open systems	The level of the self-maintaining structure. This is the level at which life begins to differentiate itself from non-life, the level of the cell. At this level the

property of self-maintenance in the midst of a throughput of material becomes of dominant importance.

Genetic-societal systems   The level of the plant. At this level there is a division of labour among cells to form a cell-society with differentiated and mutually dependent parts (roots, leaves, seeds etc.), but no highly specialized sense organs and information receptors are diffuse and incapable of much throughput of information.

Animal   This level is characterized by increased mobility, goal-seeking behaviour and self-awareness. Here we have the development of specialized information-receptors (eyes, ears, etc.) leading to an enormous increase in the intake of information; we have also a great development of nervous systems, leading ultimately to the brain, as an organizer of the information intake into a knowledge structure or 'image'.

Human   The level of the individual human being considered as a system. Here we have self-consciousness, something different from mere awareness. Man's image has a self-reflexive quality – he not only knows, but he knows that he knows. This property is probably bound up with the phenomenon of language and symbolism. Man is also distinguished from the animals by a much more elaborate image of time and relationship; he knows that he dies and contemplates in his behaviour more than a life span. He exists not only in time and space but in history.

Social   The level of social organizations. Man isolated from his fellows is practically unknown. At this level we must concern

| | ourselves with the content and meaning of messages, the nature and dimensions of value systems, the transcription of images into an historical record, the subtle symbolizations of art, music and poetry and the complexity of human emotion – human life and society in all its richness. |
| *Transcendental* | This is a remainder term to allow for more advanced systems still to be discovered and the 'inescapable unknowables'. In Boulding's words, 'it will be a sad day for man when nobody is allowed to ask questions that do not have any answers.' |

B.B.S. pointed out that the properties which distinguished each higher level from the one below it were holistic and could not have been forecast by a study of the system at the lower level. Such are the qualities of any organization/organism, or indeed any whole, which will disappear if it is subjected to analysis. Boulding himself suggests that a valuable use of his scheme is to prevent us from accepting as final a level of analysis which is below the level of the theoretical world we are investigating. Because, in a sense, each level incorporates all those below it, much valuable information and insights can be obtained by applying low-level systems to high-level subject matter. Thus most of the theoretical schemes of the social sciences were at the time of his article still at the level of the simple dynamic system just rising to that of the cybernetic system, although the subject matter is clearly at the level of social organizations. Indeed those who talk of 'models' of organizations or people have so far always produced models which themselves are systems of a very low order.

Comparing Ralph Coverdale's classification with that of Boulding, it is clear that the former was only dealing with systems at the human level. The important point his presentation draws attention to is the ill-effects of treating people: (a) as 'stuff' or 'raw material', as gunfodder, as so many units (which are seen as static); or (b) as machines capable of performing certain operations and which have in-built purpose and are dynamic but wear out and cannot adapt; or (c) as animals or organisms; rather than as (d) human beings who have ethical feelings and understanding.

Under the designation OD or organization development much work has been done within Coverdale concerned with understanding how to help those involved in organizations to be more effective at the human level.

Returning to Boulding's classification, B.B.S. pointed out that when considering closed systems we only deal with what lies within the boundary. Nothing fresh can be brought in, therefore the whole procedure is deductive in the sense that it must take place within what was available at the start. It is entirely deterministic. The laws of entropy apply and the final state of the system must be one of equilibrium with no work being possible.

With open systems, a steady state, not equilibrium can be reached; in such a state work can be done.

The distinction can be blurred as for instance where an electric clock is connected to a mains supply of electricity or perhaps better still powered by the sun. In most cases the distinction between successive levels can be blurred, e.g. social organization can be found at the animal level, but the overall picture is clear enough.

When we come to open systems we find that they draw on the environment and later emit to it. What they derive from the environment may be food, fuel, ideas or materials or, in the case of organizations, people. In general, what is drawn in is processed in some way and what is emitted is usually different from what is taken in. Where 'people' are the intake they will in general be different when they leave. (For a fuller note on open and closed systems see Appendix 2.)

B.B.S. also pointed out that, since an open system interacts with its environment, the study of environments becomes important. In a seminal article ('The Causal Texture of Organizational Environments', *Human Relations 1965*, vol. 18, pp. 21–32) Emery and Trist envisage the environment as consisting of goals. These may be independent of one another or related in various ways. Metcalfe ('Systems Models, Economic Models and the Causal Texture of Organizational Environments: An Approach to Macro-organization Theory', *Human Relations 1974*, vol. 27, pp. 631–663) builds on Emery and Trist, amending their classification of environments so as to reconcile systems theory, economic theory and organization theory.

An important point that emerges from a table in this article

('Modes of adaptation to environments of different causal textures') is that the more connections there are among the constituents in the environment, the more inclusive, extensive and complex must be the organizational responses. In the limit very richly joined environments are uncontrollable. The only hope offered is that such environments may become controllable if in some way they can be treated so as to become less richly connected.

In another important article ('Organizational Strategies and Interorganizational Structure: a Development of the Organization Set', September 1974, London Graduate School of Business Studies) Metcalfe describes some of the environments encountered in the work of Economic Development Committees and the strategies which were developed to cope with these.

He distinguishes environmental responsiveness, representing the behaviour of organizations as described by Burns and Stalker (*Management of Innovation*) from the behaviour he describes as environmental effectiveness when the (focal) organization (FO) initiates activities to bring the environment under control (achieve social integration). He suggests a number of dimensions of social integration with typical issues relevant to each and appropriate organizational strategies in each case. (*Note*: It is important to remember that the particular organizations studied, Economic Development Committees, had no power to compel or to arbitrate and had to act by persuasion and reasoning.)

1 *Cultural*– goals and values:
(a) Put forward ideology accepted by those in the organization set.
(b) Coopt more consenters until the FO is accepted.

2 *Normative*– behaviour and expectations:
(a) Ensure more members take their contribution seriously.
(b) FO is challenged. FO must be protected, invoke peer group support. This course is appropriate when principle is non-negotiable.

3 *Communicative*– mutual awareness of expectation and interests:
(a) Lack of communication. Make sure that differing demands are known and create awareness of interdependent common interests.
(b) Conflicting interests revealed.

4 *Functional–* reciprocal   (a) Differences in power: form defensive
exchange and power   coalition among the less powerful.
relations: (b) Developmental coalitions.

Further consideration of systems thinking led to some exploration to discover whether the approach of P. B. Checkland (outlined in *Systems Thinking, Systems Practice*, 1981) could be married,
welded, grafted, combined or mixed with 'Coverdale' to produce
something yet more powerful. During this exploration B.B.S. drew
attention to an article by Checkland ('Vickers' Concept of an Appreciative System: a Systemic Account', *Journal of Applied Systems
Analysis*, April 1986, vol. 13, pp. 3–18). He wrote, 'Here we meet
yet another approach or attitude and so it seems worthwhile to
attempt comparisons rather than combinations. How are they alike
and how do they differ?

'They are alike in that all three are concerned with affairs, with
things that happen or are done. All three operate in cycles, successive cycles building on their predecessors. But I think that if we were
to class them together as working with cycles, one would need to
add another term to the "preparation, action, review" of Coverdale. This is appropriate enough at the first cycle, but for successive cycles we really need another step to indicate that review has
two steps, the collection of information and the sorting of it that
leads to preparation. Incidentally if we do this doesn't it offer a link
to Kolb's four-stage cycle of learning?

'If we now turn to the effects of the different systems, as I
understand them: (a) Checkland's leads one to a progressively
fuller and more detailed layout and to a better match between the
real and the conceptual system; (b) Vickers' method leads surely to
the maintenance of desirable states; (c) Coverdale leads to getting
things done.

'Each in its way is admirable, but put this way the three do not
seem to be easily compatible.

'This finding has led me to consider another view; that each has
its use and that we may understand the relationships among them
better if we look at their origins.

'Checkland has described how he embarked on a programme of
research and if we follow his route we shall find out more and more
about systems and in more and more detail how our conceptual
world is related to the real world. Am I right in thinking that

progress will be represented by a progressively closer link between the two?

'Vickers' concepts look more reasonable and appropriate when we recall that he was by profession a solicitor and that in his long and distinguished career he served on a number of important bodies. He was well placed to view situations from Olympian heights. Like a military commander viewing patterns of flags on maps one may appreciate situations and relationships that are or are not desirable and those which should or should not be maintained.

'When Coverdale started in this field he was working with managers, and it still seems to me that managers are there to get things done. The method that has developed in Coverdale is appropriate to tactical and operational levels, where one can usefully talk of aims, proximate, intermediate or even ultimate. It is interesting to compare this practical world with that of Vickers who concerns himself with maintaining relationships; an activity which he describes as "a richer concept of human action than the popular but poverty stricken notion of goal seeking".

'Taking these three approaches there seems to be at least a prima facie case for saying that Checkland presents a system appropriate for one conducting research. His successive cycles may bring one progressively closer to formulating patterns of behaviour in the groups he observes and he describes the influences at work in the successive stages that operations go through. The approach could be applied in any field of endeavour.

'Vickers, as I understand Checkland's account, may be compared to a Cabinet Minister who may be concerned with e.g. the health of a country, or the safety of the realm, at which level reducing the cost of hospitals or production of efficient weapons can be seen as "poverty stricken goal seeking". To people at lower levels these may be seen as important and desirable goals.

'What I say must not be taken as contemptuous or dismissive; there is a place for such an approach, and that place is at the top. Having reached this point I felt inclined to say now I have related Vickers to Coverdale satisfactorily. But though "so far so good" I must go further. To take an example: if I say, "I am concerned to maintain my house" it sounds like a good Vickersian statement. But if I proceed to work out what it implies I find it can be broken down to such statements as: "The stonework, brickwork or woodwork must be sound, the windows and doors wind and watertight, so must be the roof and if possible that should be snow tight too. Then there is the plumbing and the electric wiring, and I must not forget the interior decoration.''

'If I consider all these relationships, I find that maintaining them entails doing things or having things done. Furthermore, it is important in each case to be clear about aims, and also to specify objectives. So it seems that in practice Vickers needs Coverdale: while if I had started with Coverdale I would see the advantages of introducing Vickers.

'Having got so far I find there is another set of questions to ask: "Which of the various activities involved in maintaining my house should I do first? Can I arrange them in an order so that they don't interfere with or preclude one another?" Clearly most of them can be seen as cyclical, e.g. repaint every six years or rewire after twenty. I then begin to see a Checklandian diagram taking shape with all steps being monitored by my bank statements and my wife's preferences.

'Looking at the lovely card house I have built I feel I must not attempt to add more lest it should be one card too many. So I send it to you as it is!'

24

Organizations and organizing

It is clear that as soon as the people required to tackle a situation and get things done increase in numbers and diversity of skills, knowledge and experience needed, then the question of organization beyond that necessary for a small group or team arises. In addition we tend to talk of an organization (as opposed to a group or team).

During some discussions on whether courses dealing with teams could lead naturally into courses dealing with organizations or whether there was a gulf fixed between them, so that courses dealing with organizations would require a fresh start, B.B.S. suggested that it might be useful to consider what one means by *organizing* before attempting to deal with *organizations*. Following this line of thought subsequently he made the following observations.

'I think the first point to come out is that there are plenty of activities which one would organize, without there being any suggestion of an organization e.g. a lunch with some old friends or one's reading list. We should use the word organize in the same way for the activities of a group of people, implying that they would ensure that their activities were coherent and orderly. When this is so it is almost inevitable that forethought and planning are involved to some degree.

'Approaching the matter in this way what a group on a Coverdale Part 1 course does is to organize itself (cf the term "self-regulating group" which was at one time seen as the aim of groups on Part 1). An important part of this organizing is process planning, particularly the planning of the procedures which enable people to be agreed as to how they do things.

'On Part 1 this organizing is done within itself by a group which remains the same for the duration of the course, and is not making preparation for working together subsequently. (In fact planning for future applications is on an individual basis' – when individual participants plan to apply lessons they have derived from the course experience to situations in their work.)

'In Part 2 the circumstances change. In steering and joining members make explicit preparation for working in a group after changes in its composition. They see it, or it is represented to them, as a feature of organizing themselves that they should make plans in advance of the changes.

'It seems to me that you could go on making the conditions that a group is to face more and more complicated; one would continue to talk of such a group organizing itself, and still not find oneself having to talk of an organization. If we ask what this "organizing" consists of, I think we find the crucial point to be that the group jointly sets up rules for its own behaviour and procedure, so that things may be done in an orderly way.

'The important question now is, what changes in conditions lead one to talk of an organization? (Implying I think that the concept of a self-organizing group is no longer adequate.)

'Size, internal heterogeneity and a need for durability are all relevant. Perhaps the most important is durability in the sense of persistence in spite of loss of people, and in spite of the accession of newcomers.

'Here it is useful to note the important difference between devising and setting up an organization on the one hand, and maintaining or modifying an organization on the other.

'In setting up an organization those involved can be concerned in the process planning which leads to the "rules" for procedures, but in maintaining one it is necessary to face the effects on a group of people leaving and of fresh people joining who were not involved in the design. Thus, for instance, in setting the organization up it may be agreed that certain kinds of information are to follow a particular route. But a newcomer to an existing organization is not party to such an agreement and is liable to find himself being told "this is how it is done". An obvious instance is army discipline.

'It seems then to be an important part of the design of an organization that it should provide for the proper induction of newcomers. As before with the working of a self-regulating or organizing group, such provision can be made by process planning.

'Other factors affecting the nature of the organization are numbers and the heterogeneity of functions, but when the influence of these is appreciated provision can be made by process planning.

'All I have said so far concerns the internal functioning of the group of people (of whatever size) but has taken no account of environmental influences. Organizations which made no allowance for changes in their environment would soon find themselves in difficulties. It is at this point that I find the article entitled 'Camping on Seesaws: prescriptions for self-designing organizations' by Bo L. T. Hedberg et al (*Administrative Science Quarterly*, March 1976, vol. 21) so interesting, giving six dimensions in which some degree of latitude or variability is desirable. The phrasing of the article as it stands was difficult for me; but I found the difficulties seemed to be resolved if each of his six aphorisms were seen as calling for a balance between extremes, e.g. it is important to adapt to conditions, but it is also important to remain adaptable (see aphorism number 5) which is my interpretation of Hedberg's "Improvement demands minimal consistency".

'What I see now is that any group can make provision for coping with any difficulty or change that it foresees (whether the provision would be effective is another matter). The question for an organization is how many influences it will seek to plan for, or, incorporate in its own plans. An alternative is not to make provision, but to try to deal with difficulties as they arise. If carried far, this last approach is called "crisis management"; but it may be no more desirable to try to have plans for every emergency than to do without. (Some people enjoy meeting the buffets of fortune.)

'Looked at in this way groups, teams and organizations are comparable; all involve people organizing in various ways, the differences lie in what situations they organize themselves to meet, and how extensive is the field of possibilities that they organize for. Basically the method to be adopted is the same throughout, to use process planning to produce agreed procedures.

'Returning to courses what is attempted and what the situations are change, from Part 1 where a group aims to become self-regulating (becoming a team seems to be a success criterion rather than an aim); to Part 2 where with steering and joining the field extends to include fresh people joining a group, to form a team quickly. There is a jump, though not a discontinuity, to where one is setting up an organization. There it is important to have a system which will continue to run, when those who made it leave and when new people are introduced. Among people who know each other well, it may seem obvious and common sense that A should give instructions to B and this may be incorporated in the structure; but when new recruits join the organization this arrangement may not look at all obvious or appropriate.

'It is an important feature of organizations, as here developed, that the induction of newcomers entails ensuring that they understand and accept the provisions already made (e.g. structure, channels of communication and lines of command, if they exist). It may also follow that if newcomers object to what they find their objections will be heard and considered. This situation would be, in its turn, one for which provision would need to be made.

'I have not said anything about aims or leadership; not because I think they are not important but because they will both be required by any kind or size of group and I don't at the moment see any differences except those already implied i.e. that aims of, or in, an organization will tend to be long term and that provision will be required in organizations for succession to leading positions.

'In terms of what I have said I am clear that the forms or shapes taken, appropriately, by organizations will be very variable. This situation will be further complicated if we consider that the attitude exhibited by the behaviour of an organization may tend towards improvisation, even crisis management, in one direction or towards detailed provision for all contingencies in the other (e.g. US Marines Officers tactical handbook on successive pages: page a "Crossing a river at night", page a + 1 "Crossing a river at night with mules"). I am very doubtful whether it would be possible to speak of optimum attitudes, and one must, in practice, expect great variation.'

25

Organizations and a systematic approach

Various attempts have been made to develop a model of an organization from what had been formalized into a systematic approach. In commenting on this B.B.S. wrote:

'At intervals over the years I have tried to see how S/A looks when applied in an organization rather than in a group. I first developed the theme years ago in *A Systematic Approach to Getting Things Done*, June 1965, where I described how I saw the preparation side of S/A moving from one level to another in a hierarchy. I then said in review a reverse process would take place.'

(*Note:* The above paper is reproduced in full as Appendix 1 to this book.)

'Ralph Coverdale's development of a parallel between an organization and phases of S/A was, so far as I can recall, not based on any discussion between us.

'When recently I returned to these ideas, I found that I had moved on, in a sense that I saw the procedure not depending so much on steps recognized in S/A, but rather in terms of the stages which would occur when one moved from one information level to another i.e. when fresh kinds of information were introduced; or indeed when one moved from one administrative level to another.

'Thus while it is usual to describe S/A in, say, four stages of preparation (and one in review) one might find a project or undertaking passing through many more, if there are more administrative levels. (I will not go into the question here whether one could argue that because four, say, have been found adequate for S/A only four are needed in administration.)

'The picture is reasonably clear of the content of review changing as it moves from one layer to another, for the information contributed at each level changes from one to the next in the successive stages of preparation, so it would not be surprising if the information supplied by the review differed from stage to stage.

'Will it follow that if the whole of a job or project is conducted within one group, which naturally will go through all stages of preparation in S/A, that the review will go through the successive stages *in the reverse order*?

'Turning to the review session on the 10th,' (this was a meeting of a small group of people who had organized some internal seminars for Coverdale staff) 'it was this last point which was exercising me and puzzling me: for it seemed that if this view were correct we should have begun by considering the products of the seminars and have proceeded thence to consider the plan. After that, if we viewed the whole exercise as having taken place at one level, we should have moved on to consider whether objectives were met, or whether things remained to be done. The next stage would have been to consider aims and whether progress had been made towards realizing them – or whether possibly they should be changed. It would remain to consider whether it was still desirable to devote energy and resources to these aims. Here I found difficulty again because it seemed to me that this last question would really be for the Board of the Coverdale Organisation.

'I think the foregoing should explain to some extent my difficulties on the 10th, but it remains to draw attention to one more difficulty – what kind of group were we? Were we one intermediate group in a hierarchy or were we a group conducting an exercise or project at one level? The latter does not sound realistic since the people who had actually done the work were nearly all not there, and also it is quite clear on reflection that the resources to make the work possible were not contained or controlled or made available within the group which met on the 10th.

'I find the concept of review taking the form appropriate to the level at which it is made persuasive and in principle helpful; I admit it tied me up at our meeting, but this was I think largely because I had not had a chance to talk about it with anyone before we began.'

26

Organization development

An earlier chapter discussed the development of teams; it may be useful now to look at the development of organizations and what similarities and differences exist. Both are set up to get things done, and this must be kept firmly in mind when considering the development of either. Since some coordination of thinking and action is needed in both, encouraging teamwork in the sense of effective cooperation among those involved is important in both. However, as pointed out in Chapter 24 on organizations and organizing, 'organizations' tend to be distinguished from 'teams' by size, heterogeneity and, in particular, durability. The greater numbers of people involved, the greater number and diversity of elements and functions internally, the greater number and diversity of transactions with the environment and the need for durability despite changes both in composition of people internally and changes in the outside environment, are all factors which make the development of an organization a much larger task than the development of a small group or team.

However, it is not difficult to see how in general the same concepts and principles apply, providing they can be brought to bear. With both small groups or teams and organizations it is relevant to consider what is being done and how in all its aspects. With both it is important to ensure common comprehension of aims, coordination of thought and effort, provision of steering and leadership as appropriate, the maintenance of awareness through observation of what and how things are happening and the use of the fruits of observation as a basis for making process plans to improve performance.

The whole idea of developing organizations and of 'organization development' as described in the literature arose originally out of small group work, largely in the USA. B.B.S. noted that when he went to the States in 1967 to study 'the implications of small group work for organization theory' he met OD flourishing. It was based on sensitivity training and 'T' groups. Of the term OD it was said, 'you can't go to people and say I will change your organization; you can go and say I will help you to develop it.' So OD was aimed at change. There was, however, beginning to be a realization that sensitivity training and 'T' groups were not (after all) panaceas for management difficulties.

Subsequently the term OD has become used freely but is imprecise. (Some years ago the Director of Training, Training Services Agency in the UK said he had come across eighteen different definitions.) Indeed since almost all the vast number of books and articles on the topic have been written not by businessmen or others actually involved in running large organizations but by consultants and academics they tend to focus on methods to promote change in an organization in the direction of a 'climate' seen as desirable by the writer.

In considering a number of accounts of consultancy work in the field of OD carried out by Coverdale staff B.B.S. commented that he had 'tried to discover common principles underlying the advice and the structural trees or patterns of organization which emerged.

'Except that in a number of cases better business results and better human relationships were achieved, I cannot so far discover common features. Maybe I haven't tried hard enough. I felt that what was emerging was a view that underlying the success of Coverdale consultancy was the attitude and approach of their consultants. Their evident honesty, sincerity and desire to help generate in clients a confidence in them which contributes to the planning and implementation of changes. Such a situation is commendable up to a point, but it is insecure, for clients may ask, "What are you aiming at?" I don't think it is good enough to say that aims depend on circumstances, unless you can add principles on which your work is based. Another answer to a client could be, it is your aims which matter not the consultant's. In one organization, the drive to increase business seemed to stem from anxiety among employees lest jobs be lost. In another, loss of jobs on a considerable scale seems to have been accepted.

'Methods often described under the heading OD are concerned with the way the processes of a consultancy are carried out, in other words how you introduce advice and control the spread of ideas; they are not concerned with aims or with what is being put over, they don't give any idea of content or what you are trying to achieve – they could be used equally well for expansion or contraction.

'In discussion it has been pointed out that there are different ideas as to what an organization should be like. It is clear, moreover, that organizations differ one from another and I think it follows that aims or methods useful for one could be disastrous for another. J. R. Galbraith in a book called *Designing Complex Organizations* has a section where he considers the courses of action that would be appropriate for a firm where business is slack and where products are piling up. He proposed:

1 Methods which will reduce pressure: (a) by producing less and making less effort to sell; or (b) by delegating parts to independent units.
2 Methods which will help by increasing business: (a) by ensuring greater flow of information vertically within the organization by installing computers – this may be expensive; or (b) by increasing lateral communications, e.g. by setting up a matrix organization.

'Emery and Trist (*Human Relations 1965*, vol. 18, pp. 21–32) have drawn attention to the effects of an environment in an organization. They consider a range of environments and describe for each of four types, the kind of activity which will be required of an organization in them.

'Metcalfe (*Human Relations 1974*, vol. 27, pp. 639–663) from a somewhat different point of view describes the qualities of a range of environments and the kind of strategy appropriate to bringing an organization and its environment into cooperation.

'In both cases it looks as if the environment can be described and even the description "turbulent" does not suggest that one may face change of conditions. This point is, however, predominant in Hedberg's strange and interesting "Camping on Seesaws" (*Administrative Science Quarterly*, March 1976, vol. 21), where the theme throughout is that for an organization to be self-organizing it must have within itself variety of various kinds so that it can produce appropriate responses in the face of changing circumstances. (Is this in a way similar to the idea of maintaining varieties of plants, or animals, which do not appear to be immediately useful so as to preserve a genetic bank of chromosomes which will allow fresh varieties to be bred to meet changing needs?)'

Building on his suggestion that it was fruitful first to look at 'organi*zing*' rather than 'organiz*ations* (see Chapter 24), B.B.S.

noted, 'if one is to ask questions to find out how he or they should organize their affairs, we must find out first how they do so *now*.... If you can obtain these answers' (in respect to a number of different facets of present ways of organizing) 'the next step, if you are concerned with organizing, should be to ask something like, "What do you organize your affairs like this *for*?" i.e. what influences, events, eventualities, do you work or attempt to forestall or palliate, or bring or keep under control?

'I would like to think that the approach to order and control by way of organizing, (in other words "what do you do?"), will lead to a fresh approach and throw fresh light on ideas about structure and operation. I must, however, admit that this seems to be asking a lot of people who have developed and run businesses perhaps of great size and perhaps with considerable success. It is also a bit difficult to talk of a fresh look, when there are in existence quite a number of theories of organization.'

In illustration of this last point he drew attention to an editorial by Samuel Eilon from *Omega*, vol. 9, no. 3 (1981), which included a list of some ten existing theories of organization and even then ended 'and so on'.

B.B.S. continued, 'What I should be inclined to look for would be an approach based on an exercise from one of the first two Avoncroft courses,' (these were the first courses run by Coverdale and Babington Smith at the Steel Company of Wales), 'where three groups were each invited to produce a statement of sound principles of management, one being based on the overriding principle that profits must be maximized, the second on the overriding principle that relationships among staff and management should be optimized and the third that maximum efficiency was to be sought.

'If you were dealing with completely mechanical systems the first and third of these could be unchanged while the second would become something like "minimize breakdowns and maintenance". If, however, you are dealing with human beings, it looks necessary to introduce ethical considerations. I shall return to this point briefly later.

'In the course of recent reading I have come across a book with some interesting points about the development of small firms. It is called, believe it or not, *Spring Onions* (Faber and Faber 1942), sub-title, "The autobiography of Duncan McGuffie". In this book McGuffie writes "I made a list of resolutions to be read out at every annual meeting. At first I thought they should be the articles of association, but the solicitor firmly (and rightly) insisted that they should go in the minute book. Here they are:

1 The maintenance of a policy of offering for sale sound goods only.
2 That all employees shall be paid the highest wages possible consistent with the proper management of the Company.
3 That all employees shall be treated and regarded as fellow-workers.
4 That the Company shall specialize in one particular crop or line of business and shall grow only such other subsidiary crops as are essential for the well-being of the special crop or develop only such subsidiary lines of business as are essential for such principal line of business.
5 Reasonable holidays shall be taken by all members of the staff yearly.
6 The directors, managers and foreman shall give to those working under them as much responsibility as they are capable of bearing.
7 In the conduct of the Company's affairs national interests shall be placed before the Company's immediate interests and in all circumstances the best possible service to the nation shall be rendered by the Company."'

B.B.S. continued, 'Would such a set of resolutions as given above constitute an organization or would you need to ask next, "How will you ensure that these are applied?" a question which will lead in turn to, "Will you need a set of procedures to ensure that they are applied?" If one had answers to these what more would be needed for an organization?

'In *Futures Research: New Directions* edited by Linstone and Simmonds (Addison Wesley 1977) there is an interesting chapter by Sir Geoffrey Vickers on the future of culture. At one stage he says, "Central to the culture of every tribe ever explored by an anthropologist are its answers to two questions: Who is my neighbour? and What is my duty to him? The wider the definition of neighbour the greater – and usually also the more conflicting – becomes the load of duties, even if the duties themselves do not increase in variety." (See my earlier point about ethical considerations.)'

An early chapter in this book on purpose and choice pointed out that people involved in any joint enterprise can choose to help or hinder each other – and that choice is always open. Anyone within an organization can be regarded as involved in a joint enterprise with his immediate colleagues, boss and subordinates, with people in other departments in the same organization, with suppliers, with customers, with the community at large. Transactions take place between people internally and across the boundary of the organization with suppliers, customers, the community in its environment. In developing an organization the choice can be made how far to extend the definition of 'neighbour' in encouraging those transactions to be mutually beneficial. It is obvious that the wider the view taken by the majority of people in respect to their *internal* transactions the better their cooperation is likely to be in working towards the organization's objectives. However, organizations are 'open' systems in that they draw on their environment (materials, services, ideas, information, people) and emit to it (goods, services, ideas, information, people). Thus they interact with their environment and there are many transactions that cross the boundary of the organization. Such transactions can be more or less efficient and more or less mutually beneficial. It can reasonably be argued that, in the long run, unless they are perceived as to some extent both efficient *and* mutually beneficial by those involved internally *and* in the external environment they will not continue to be effective, if indeed they continue at all. The development of any organization must of necessity take into account its many different transactions with its environment, the nature of that environment, how the environment itself is changing and what can be done to influence it.

27

Boards of directors

As has been pointed out in earlier chapters the ideas which are the subject of this book started from a point where Coverdale was working with middle management. The approach developed was seen as particularly appropriate at that level. As B.B.S. has commented, 'by 1965 we had noted that what would help senior management would differ from what helped middle management, but that what the difference was remained unclear. (The descriptions I tried were completely inward-looking.)'

Subsequently, as he observed, courses were run for directors, but these remained largely concerned with operations *internal* to an organization. While it is clear that a major part of the work of directors will be directed outwards and not lie within their organizations, it may be useful to draw attention to those ideas contained in earlier chapters that are of relevance.

Boards of directors can be regarded in the same way as any small group or team insofar as their internal proceedings and their own immediate transactions across the boundary of their own group are concerned. Thus there is little to add on these topics to what has been said in earlier chapters, since the same issues, concepts and principles apply. What distinguishes their work is the situations they, and the people under them, organize to meet and the extensiveness of the field of possibilities they can organize for. Size, heterogeneity and in particular durability are what tend to distinguish 'organizations' from teams or small groups. It is these which affect the nature and type of planning which boards of directors need to undertake. While it may be unwise to attempt to plan for every eventuality, any organization where no planning is done or initiated by the board in some essential areas is likely to get into difficulties.

In considering what those essential areas are it is helpful to keep in mind that an organization can be regarded as an 'open' system for getting things done. As with individuals and small groups concerned with getting things done there is a need for observation, for reviewing and attempting to adjust or improve both what is being done and how (means and resources, methods, human interaction). To be confident that any organization is working effectively it follows that a board will need to ensure that both what and how in all its aspects are monitored and adjustments made as necessary.

What is done by and in an organization is a function of the aims being pursued and the understanding and commitment of those contributing to their achievement. People in most organizations are arranged in a hierarchical structure. Prime issues for any board are how aims, criteria and priorities are communicated down the structure, how information, views and ideas are communicated up and across the structure and how common understanding, commitment and contribution are encouraged at all levels. We have referred above to 'the aims being pursued'. It is of course the function of a board to ensure these are set as well as communicated, progress monitored and adjustments made. Setting of aims involves choice and, since organizations are part of larger communities of people, that choice is affected by ethical considerations. Indeed a major difference between people at different levels in an organization is that the prime concerns at the bottom tend to be with fairness and being treated fairly, in the middle with loyalty and giving and receiving loyalty, and at the top with ethics and choice.

If we turn from what is done to how, then again it would seem clear that boards need to ensure that resources (including the knowledge, skills and experience of people) are used effectively throughout the organization and that this is dependent on maintaining a flow of information to monitor performance. In addition, securing and developing resources and maintaining an appropriate balance between resources available and achievements sought are important matters for any board. So, too, are the methods adopted, the procedures used and the human interaction both internally and across the boundary of the organization. As with communication of aims and information, the factors of size, heterogeneity and durability which distinguish an organization from a small group increase the difficulties of ensuring common understanding of methods, procedures and principles of behaviour throughout the levels of the structure.

One would hesitate to prescribe ways in which boards should attempt to deal with such difficulties. Nevertheless, if plans are to be made, some general points seem clear. The plans will need to make provision for, in addition to the personal example set by board members in their own behaviour, a combination of statements of policy (or what some companies describe as company philosophy) which are disseminated throughout the organization and the implementation of some system of training.

In Chapter 26 on developing organizations there is quoted what amounts to a 'company philosophy' for a very small firm. In practice it can be seen as a set of rules to guide action when choice arises. It is noticeable that this short list contains not only statements about *what* the organization is *for* (what business it is *in*) but about treatment of members or internal relationships and about relationships with the external environment (the sort of organization the owner wants it to be). Indeed, as pointed out in Chapter 26, one way of thinking about an organization is as a system of transactions for getting things done. These transactions include those between the organization and its environment (customers, suppliers, the community), those between the various individuals and groups of individuals within it, those between the organization and individual employees. Establishing and disseminating a set of resolutions or policy like that above is one step towards guiding behaviour in those transactions.

A second logical step for a board is to consider how to ensure these are applied; this in turn would seem to lead to the necessity for (a) procedures to ensure application of policies and (b) some sort of training to familiarize newcomers with both procedures and policies.

As noted earlier, perhaps the most important distinguishing feature of 'organizations' is their need for durability, to be able to persist in effectiveness of operation in spite of the loss of people and in spite of the accession of newcomers. In considering the part of a system of training in contributing to this, as B.B.S. pointed out when seeking the warrant for management training, there seem to be two obvious stages and a third not so obvious which is of very great importance because, if it is included, there is a system which is in a sense self-regulating and self-perpetuating, thus giving a powerful form of continuity to an organization which adopts it.

The first stage of such a system of training is to ensure that newcomers become acquainted with the procedures of the organization and adopt good habits. What such habits are depends on the nature of the enterprise but it seems self-evident that an organization of any size will benefit if all its employees are taught or learn to do things in certain ways. (We are referring here to the needs for those joining an existing organization. However, it also seems self-evident that, where a top management or board of directors wishes to bring about changes in the climate or culture of an organization this may require changes in procedures and in principles of operation and behaviour which will also have to be introduced and 'taught' in some way to existing staff.)

As a second stage of the system, once employees have developed habits and become used to operating procedures, they need to be called upon to think, to stir up their ideas which may have settled into clichés and, by considering those habits in the setting of actual experience, to learn what is useful about them and what may be discarded or developed. The learning in this stage is different from being taught in the first since it carries with it some understanding of the principles involved i.e. the training or learning experience should be designed to enable participants to take a fresh look at how they manage and to attempt to develop principles to guide their behaviour when faced with unexpected difficulties.

The third stage in a complete system of training involves periodic conferences at which senior management have the opportunity to be informed of the current training procedures adopted with their juniors, to comment on and to contribute to these in the light of their own experience.

To summarize the particular part which boards of directors or people at the top of an organization seem to need to play in respect to their work within the organization, the concerns peculiar to them are with:

1 Choice of aims, especially long term, to be pursued.
2 Ensuring that aims, criteria and priorities are communicated, observation is maintained and information is fed back through the levels of the structure.
3 Ensuring that principles of operation, including of behaviour, are clarified and applied throughout the organization to guide interaction internally and with the environment.
4 Ensuring plans are made and implemented to maintain the durability of the organization in the face of changes in personnel

through loss and accession, and in the face of changes in the external environment. Since for a board such plans will be long term, it is more usual to refer to them as 'strategies'.

In respect to their dealings with the environment and the kind of training experience that would help them in these, B.B.S. has suggested that there seem to be two complementary activities: (a) gaining and assimilating information (observation in a broad sense) and (b) making interventions – these may be very different from those made within.

Earlier, in Chapter 26 on developing organizations Sir Geoffrey Vickers was quoted, 'Central to the culture of every tribe ever explored by an anthropologist are its answers to two questions: Who is my neighbour? and What is my duty to him? The wider the definition of neighbour the greater – and usually also the more conflicting – becomes the load of duties, even if the duties themselves do not increase in variety.' In the same chapter it was also pointed out that people involved in any joint enterprise can choose to help or hinder each other – and that choice is always open. Anyone within an organization can be regarded as involved in a joint enterprise with his immediate colleagues, boss and subordinates, with people in other departments in the same organization, with suppliers, with customers and with the community at large. Transactions take place between people within the organization and across the boundary of the organization with suppliers, customers and the environment.

In providing direction to an organization, boards of directors can make the choice how far to extend the definition of 'neighbour' in encouraging those transactions to be mutually beneficial. It is obvious that the wider the view taken by the majority of people in respect to their *internal* transactions the better their cooperation is likely to be in working towards the organization's objectives. However, organizations are 'open' systems in that they draw on their environment (materials, services, ideas, information, people) and emit to it (goods, services, ideas, information, people). Thus they interact with their environment and there are many transactions that cross the boundary of the organization. Unless such transactions are perceived as to some extent both efficient and mutually beneficial by those involved internally and in the external environment, it is difficult to see how an organization can be effective. In running and developing any organization boards of directors must of necessity take into account its many different transactions with its environment, the nature of that environment, how the environment itself is changing and what can be done to influence it.

28

Systematic approach – possible developments

As early as 1967, in a talk given to an international seminar held at Trinity College, Dublin, B.B.S. pointed out, 'Coverdale Training is not a package deal in the sense that there is a system which you can learn and then say, "Now I know it all". If you embark on it, you embark on a continuing process. There is no finality in a systematic approach to getting things done. If you persist in it, I believe you will get things done and that you will continue to make discoveries.'

The earlier chapters have attempted to trace the development of ideas, as discoveries have been made. The majority of these ideas have been incorporated into the body of methods still known as Coverdale Training. Those methods have grown over the years and their application has widened to areas well beyond those where the original ideas emanated, although their connection with the roots remains clear. At intervals B.B.S. has drawn attention to the importance of going back to those roots in trying to ensure that principles and methods developed in one setting are not simply assumed to apply in other settings without due consideration. There are many examples in the body of the text. This final chapter provides one or two other examples and suggests possible future developments.

In 1985 B.B.S. wrote a personal account of the origins, development and status of a systematic approach to getting things done. Material from this account has been used in some of the earlier chapters. After presenting his personal account at a Coverdale seminar, other points came to mind, some related to developments over the years, others to possible future developments.

'In some approaches to group work very great stress is laid on the "here and now", Coverdale by contrast lays great stress on "aims" and where are you going? As we live we move in time, and emphasis on "here and now" is incompatible with change. I think that the Heisenberg Principle of Uncertainty holds that you cannot determine, simultaneously, where a particle is *and* how fast it is moving. I also think that, if you change the terms slightly, determining precisely where a group is will leave you completely in the dark as to where it is going and as to how fast it is moving. Coverdale, from the earliest stages has been concerned with doing things and with action, hence the inappropriateness of concern with the "here and now".

'Another matter that calls for a few words was drawn to my attention during some discussions on negotiation. Someone pointed out that if you considered the "scale of degrees of agreement" from complete agreement at one end through indifference to complete disagreement at the other, one could see that a systematic approach could be usefully applied in the positive half of the scale, i.e. in a group where there is at least some agreement as to aim. On the other hand, if there is no agreement as to aim or there is active disagreement, then a systematic approach cannot be applied. It was proposed, however, that in those cases negotiation would be possible and appropriate. This might be compared to mapping the far side of the moon!

'There is something else that caused a fair amount of discussion at the time. In the late 1960s/early 1970s there was a period where groups at the start of a Part 1 course were invited to "evolve a methodical approach".' (This was said at the time to have arisen because of an expressed criticism that Coverdale emphasized the value of inductive learning yet taught a systematic approach!). 'As the course proceeded, methods were compared and a systematic approach was introduced to give groups a uniform product.

'It was found that some groups became enamoured of their own method and were reluctant to admit that the staff presentation of a systematic approach had advantages, or even that it was as good as their own. It was judged, eventually, that the disruption and diversity introduced by groups devising their own methods outweighed the value to a group of working with their own product. The practice was abandoned, but the fact that it was tried is a stage in the development of a systematic approach that should not be forgotten.

'Next there has been the question whether a systematic approach to getting things done is appropriate when senior managers or directors of an organization are involved. A systematic approach to getting things done was devised and so called when Ralph Coverdale was working almost entirely with middle management. Here the concept of getting things done still seems appropriate.

'When, however, the field of operation extends to research workers, to ministers of religion, to directors of great organizations, the title may seem and may become less appropriate. It has been said, for example, that the message coming from directors has been that methods learnt on courses have been found beneficial within their organizations but not in their dealings outside. On a much more humble level, it has been suggested that in rural communities the situations are seldom those that require prompt action and that the function of the meetings for the members of the committee is to offer opportunities for social intercourse. Members of the medical profession may well find on occasion that the urgency implied by a systematic approach to getting things done is not what is required of them.

'Recent thought about this has emphasized that the name was devised over twenty years ago and that it was time that it was looked at again. "Getting things done" was highly appropriate to middle managers in 1965, but people well outside that category have made contact with Coverdale work and it is, at least, worthwhile to consider what other terms might be useful.

'One might be concerned with, for example:

(a) Thinking things out
(b) Devising computer programs
(c) Operating on the stock market
(d) Composing music
(e) Advising busy people
(f) Deceiving one's opponents
(g) Ensuring profits
(h) Driving rivals out of business
(i) Utter destruction of enemies
(j) Peaceful coexistence
(k) Socialist Utopia
(l) Reconciliation with God
(m) Writing verse
(n) Writing fiction
(o) Learning a language

'There is of course a sense in which one may say of each of these terms, there is something to be done. But if one asks, for any one of them, what values would be involved, the portmanteau phrase "getting things done" lacks the appropriate flavour that is required. In some "speed" and "time" are important, in others precision or accuracy, in others ethical values may top the list. In others again values may be primarily personal and internal, or contrariwise, social and relational as in peaceful coexistence.

'From these considerations it seems to follow that in any case the succession of appropriate steps might be the same, but that, for instance, what was appropriate "information" or "action" might be very different. If this approach is warranted, there is obviously an enormous opening up of the field.

'So now we find that a systematic approach might be to any one of a number of topics, or should one call them objectives? But once we start changing the values involved we must as well consider whether a systematic approach is inevitably the most appropriate. There might be situations where some other kind of approach would be preferable, perhaps random or intuitive or impetuous. Once started on this line, why not creative, aggressive, pacific, honest, duplicitous, industrious, frivolous, casual, meticulous, meretricious, precipitous, circumspect, or simply courageous? I need not go on. The field is worth exploring.

'But can one suppose that one will always be able to *describe* the method adopted? It seems that whatever one does, one must do it in *some* way.

'Another picture is evoked by situations where senior managers or directors of organizations are involved. A comment that came back from someone who had taken part in such a course was that what they had learnt was of use to them within their organizations when they returned to them, but it did not help them in matters that arose in operating outside them.

'The picture that this suggested was that of a fish in a fishbowl, where there are two different worlds involved, what is in the bowl and what is outside. Perhaps fish in a river would be better, for what happens in the river produces situations of one kind, while events outside, such as the presence of birds of prey or fishermen, produce a different set. Moreover, the further down in the river the fish is, the less can it see of what is outside.

'If we try to apply this analogy, it may lead to considering different types of course, one for those whose world is largely, if not entirely, within the river, and another for those who can see out and whose course of action needs to be influenced by what can be seen.'

Appendix 1

In describing how he came to write the paper on the following pages, B.B.S. said, 'Ralph Coverdale in his courses had, from the start, emphasized the importance of thinking, and especially inductive thinking, for he was strongly of the opinion that inductive learning was a better way to learn than by being given information.

'As the approach evolved several terms were introduced for it, such as "inductive learning" and "cover learning", cover being an acronym using the initial letters of words representing five successive stages. In 1965 Seamus Roche wrote from Ireland suggesting that, whatever the title, it should indicate what the method was for. This led me to write the following paper and to give it its title.

'I still recall the pleased reception my manuscript was given at the typing bureau and the recipient's exclamation, "A systematic approach to getting things done! That sounds interesting!"'

(*Note* The paper is reproduced exactly as written in 1965, when the use of 'men' in the sense of 'people' was customary and would not have occasioned comment.)

A Systematic Approach To Getting Things Done
(Bernard Babington Smith, June 1965)

I 1 Organizations have aims, which may be changed or develop in time.
   2 What organizations can do in pursuance of aims depends in great part on the men involved and available resources.
   3 When a man joins an organization a mutual obligation is established; on the man to further the interests of the organization, and on the organization to enable the man to realize his potential.
   4 (a) Under stable conditions an organization may expect a man to improve his performance, as time passes, by practice, growing experience and diligence, for which im-

provement a man may expect due reward. (b) Where, however, discontinuous change takes place (e.g. where new inventions, new industrial processes and political changes occur) a man's work may undergo discontinuous change. In such cases the onus shifts to the organization to prepare or train him to meet the new conditions. A particular instance of such discontinuous change in a man's work and responsibilities occurs in connection with promotion. Herein lies the warrant for managerial training. In practice there may be considerable overlap between conditions 4(a) and 4(b).

II It is a truism that all business involves action.

1 It is a matter of observation that where a man sets about doing something on the basis of an instruction received he may (a) carry it out satisfactorily or (b) carry it out inappropriately because conditions have changed or (c) be unable to carry it out because of mental, physical or emotional barriers. In order to carry out an instruction appropriately he must know enough of the object of the plan and the reasons for it. Through knowing nothing of the background, he may misunderstand the instruction.

2 Since action or activities, even if they seem unique, *may* recur, it is important that note be taken of the effects of action. Where this is done learning by experience may take place. Action will therefore be incomplete unless the results are observed. Instructions must cover both steps. For jobs to be done intelligently the men involved in action and in subsequent observation should take part in the preparation of the plans.

3 A plan is a set of instructions which, if carried out, produces a desired result. (a) If a man is to understand a plan he must take part in the making of it. (b) There are apparent exceptions to this where men are trained to carry out instructions of recognizable types.

4 Once a problem has been specified (or a desired result has been stated), a plan can be made for producing the desired result. (a) It is a matter of observation that if a man be given a fully-specified problem (or a desired result) and be told to set about making a plan for it, he can only do so intelligently and appropriately if he knows something of the

reasoning and the information behind the problem, and the purpose for which the result is desired. (b) When observing results, in order to collect what is relevant a man must know what information is needed. The collection of data is not an end in itself.

5 (a) Those who are concerned with the setting of objectives (and stating desired results) do so in relation to aims and strategies, but they can only do so realistically in terms of available manpower and other resources (see I(2) above). (b) Similarly, those who are concerned to evaluate information about the effects of action can only do so with a knowledge both of the methods employed in collecting the information and the purposes for which evaluation is needed.

6 Taken in the appropriate order these steps are seen as a systematic approach to getting things done. Thus, given an aim, it is necessary: (a) To collect relevant information. (b) To decide, in terms of aim and information, what has to be done. (c) To make a plan for doing it. (d) To do it. (e) To collect information about the results of action. (f) To evaluate the information. (g) To draw lessons from the information, then lessons are incorporated in the relevant information available where fresh or further action is required. The process is called a systematic approach because it is envisaged that going through the steps outlined will leave one better able to do the job by following through the steps again which will leave one better able to do the job ... and so on. Three cases need to be considered. In repetitive tasks step (g) leads directly into step (a) for a second attempt and so on. Where a first attempt is not successful and a second or further attempts are needed – again step (g) leads directly into step (a). Where the task seems unique, in which case it is still important to complete (g) so as to be ready should the situation recur.

III Any man may consider his activities in the light of the foregoing and may adopt a systematic approach to his affairs. Frequently, however, men operate together in groups: (a) because there is too much work for one to do or (b) because there are too many kinds of work to be done or (c) because they feel safer working in a group. (It may be held that men, whatever they do, interact with others and that in this sense men may always be regarded as operating in groups.) It is a matter of observation that where a group of men set about getting something done they do not all set about it in the same way. They differ in outlook, in past experience, and in the skills they have developed.

1　The work of a group of men is more effective when their efforts are coordinated and they become a team in the sense that: (a) they share a common aim; (b) they differentiate the jobs to be done; (c) they allocate or undertake the various jobs appropriately (this includes leading and being led and zones of responsibility).

2　For this state to be achieved men must: (a) Achieve common comprehension of an aim. *This does not imply conformity, but voluntary acceptance of something understood;* (b) know enough of one another for work to be distributed appropriately.

3　2(a) and 2(b) imply the building of a body of common experience. As stated above, men develop their own methods of working. In a group differences of emphasis or outlook are almost invariably found and lead to misunderstandings. Thus some are eager to go into action while others will only move when absolutely sure of what has to be done. Others again are mines of information but not good at planning, and many will cheerfully decide what to do without making provision for review of effects afterwards. To form a team it is not enough that all should have similar training or education. Men must have the experience of doing things together in circumstances which allow observation and communication to take place. Nor is it enough to allow observation. A man must also find out how to observe and what to look and listen for.

4　(a) A man trained in observation sees and hears more than an untrained. (b) It takes time for any observer to understand what is going on in a group. It is a matter of experience that an observer goes through a succession of stages when observing others in action: (i) He can produce a narrative of successive events. (ii) With increasing acquaintance the narrative becomes fuller, and more descriptive of individual behaviour. (iii) Regularities and changes are noticed (this can only apply as instances multiply) and he begins to make comments. Comment is made where attention is drawn to regularities or changes and/or where inferences are drawn from observations. (iv) Patterns of behaviour are recognized and a descriptive framework is built. (v) Principles may be enunciated – some may take causal form. (vi) Eventually perhaps a theory may be developed.

5   Training makes a great difference to what a man can observe of what is done in a group. But whether they are trained to observe or not, men interact with each other by listening, support, encouragement, hindrance and so on, and they form impressions of each other. It is important that these interactions and impressions should be brought into the open and appreciated. Even when they have been noted, doing this requires courage and mutual confidence. Few things are more valuable to a group than that its members have the courage to tell each other matters which call for courage in the telling! With frankness and courage go confidence; with confidence in each other, courage and frankness are generated.

6   In any activity one may distinguish: (a) the task: or *what* is to be done; (b) the process: or how the task is to be done (i.e. all the various aspects of the way in which it is carried out). The process may be subdivided into: (i) the means – equipment, tools, etc., e.g. whether a job is to be done manually or by machine; (ii) the method – the way in which it is to be done, e.g. whether steps in a systematic approach are overstressed or skimped; (iii) where a group is concerned the human interaction involved. It is a matter of observation that a due balance must be preserved among these aspects of an activity. Undue emphasis on completing a task tends to mean that the processes of doing it are neglected, and the quality and even the completion itself may be affected: similarly undue attention to the processes may easily affect the completion of the task and the standard of work.

7   In a group of men, the formation of a team for a particular purpose can be brought about through the growth of common experience involved in working together, and by achieving common comprehension of aim. The development of the group depends on getting to know each other

well enough to know how best to employ the members of
the group. To see a man doing the same things repeatedly
will allow the construction of a good picture of how this
man will do this thing: it is a matter of observation that one
learns more of a man if one sees him in a variety of
situations. For a team to perform well the members must
achieve cooperation, develop the appropriate skills and
set themselves a good standard of achievement. Success
as a team for one particular purpose does not ensure good
performance on some other task. It is a very mature group
which can form an effective team for *any* task.

8   The systematic approach may be applied to any aspect of a
task. Process issues, as well as task issues, may be tackled
in this way. In groups process issues often relate to difficulties due to a man's habit of work or someone's established outlook. (a) Where such difficulties in applying a
systematic approach to a task are recognized they may be
overcome by deliberate avoidance. Sometimes, however,
difficulties recur, even where those concerned decide to
avoid them. It will then be necessary to devise systems of
procedure to prevent recurrence. (b) Process issues relating to human interaction, such as long-standing dislikes
and mistrusts, may be openly raised and faced, so long as
there is mutual confidence. (*Note*: This leaves untouched
situations where mutual confidence is lacking. Confidence
cannot be commanded. It may be *generated* by A with B by
A's assigning something to B to carry out which B com-
pletes successfully; A and B may generate mutual confidence by jointly facing and overcoming some difficulty).

IV   As a group develops *structure* is liable to emerge. Structure, as
used here, is a very general term implying relatively stable
relationships usually of a procedural nature, but when it
exists it does not necessarily define or determine the influence
exerted or initiative displayed by individuals.

1   One of the objectives of this work is to coordinate influence
and initiative with structure, not to suggest that structure
can be dispensed with. One common form of structure
may be called hierarchical, a term which implies a succession of levels through which authority flows and responsibility changes progressively. In I(3) reference was

made to a mutual obligation between an organization and a man who joined it. In some degree this mutual obligation exists between two men at different levels in the same chain of command.

2   A model of operation in a hierarchical structure has been derived in terms of a systematic approach to getting things done as shown in Figure A1.1.

Consider a hierarchical organization such as that illustrated in Figure A1.1, in which communication may flow up or down, while authority flows downwards, and in which A, B, C are the directors. (a) Suppose that A has an aim for the organization. A needs then to set or specify the problem; in other words he needs to determine what has to be done. To this end he proposes his aim to 1, 2 or 3 next to him in the organization. He must clearly supplement the statement of aim with enough information (ideas and relevant facts) while 1, 2 and 3 must also contribute relevant information (such as existing commitments, availability of resources etc.) As the group (A/123) collect and consider the evidence, what has to be done will become clearer. When A/123 can agree and state 'what has to be done' the problem is set. That this is so can be checked by stating what achievement would constitute success. This statement may be called a success criterion. (To some extent the order in which 'the problem' and 'success criteria' are introduced is not crucial, there is an advantage in ensuring that a stated problem can be replaced by a satisfactory success criterion and vice versa. The main difference may be that several success criteria may be seen independently. It is when they are taken together that

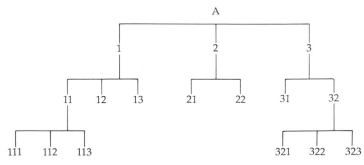

Figure A1.1

'what has to be done' can be specified.) (b) When agreement is reached in (A/123) 1 and/or 2 and/or 3 take the problem to their subordinates. Now consider the group(1/11, 12, 13); taking the problem brought by 1, the group considers *how* 'what has to be done' can be done. In other words (1/11, 12, 13) make a plan for doing 'what has to be done'. For present purposes a plan may be defined as a set of instructions, which, if carried out, will ensure the doing of 'what has to be done'. It is important to recognize that, as setting the problem was a joint enterprise for A and 1 and 2 and 3, so making a plan is a joint enterprise for 1 and 11 and 12 and 13, and relevant information or questions may be contributed by anyone in the group. The test of a plan is that any relevant question is answered by the instructions of which it is composed (see the definition of a plan above). (c) Armed with a plan in the form of a set of instructions 11, or 12, or 13 as appropriate, may either carry them out or pass them to a subordinate, say 113 to be carried out. If the plan is satisfactory 113 will have no unanswered questions. (d) When the plan is put into action, the assessment of effects begins. It is by no means certain in industrial or commercial (or indeed in many other) settings that whoever acts will also be able to observe the effects of his own actions or their effects. It looks as if, in general, someone else must make the observations. Thus if 113 acts, 323 (say) from a different group may observe and record. In general, there will be a number of observations which will need to be collected. In principle, collected observations will need to be collated and summarized; inferences will then be drawn and conveyed back to the author of the 'aim'. The aim may need to be modified before there is a fresh decision as to what has to be done leading to fresh plans. (e) The three important features of this system are: (i) that at each stage, when a group of structure $(x/x_1x_2x_3)$ functions, there must be contributions from upper and lower strata and the outcome must be understood and agreed jointly; (ii) that the chain or sequence leading to action need not be the same chain as leads from action to lessons drawn. (But if the *action* required should itself be *'observation'* – as for example where the group concerned is from a Statistical Department where their action is gathering information on the effects of actions taken by others – then the two chains may be the same); (iii) while successive stages leading to action go down the hierarchy, successive stages dealing with observation go up it; (iv) there are two corollaries: first that the pattern of organization described above implies moving from one stratum to the next at each stage. The successive stages could (and often do) take place within the same *two* levels throughout, but the pattern described brings out more clearly the principle that the two strata make different contributions at each transition. Second the case may also be envisaged where a plan or set of instructions having been agreed, they are given directly to a person to carry out, (as for instance when an order is given in the armed forces). When this occurs it seems to be implied that the recipient of the instructions has had enough training and/or experience, to understand precisely what they mean and what he has to do. Again when a man gives an order to one of his subordinates, he should know which of them it is appropriate to give it to.

3 The application of a systematic approach in a group often leads to process difficulties: a situation at least as common in hierarchical groups as in others. There seems no reason why process issues relating to the systematic approach should not be dealt with in such a group. They may be dealt with as any issue relating to a task may be dealt with. If, however, process issues involving human interaction arise in such a group there may be additional difficulties. As suggested above, provided the members of the group trust one another difficulties may be brought into the open and dealt with. If trust is missing in a hierarchical situation the matter can be altogether more awkward, for lack of trust precludes the open discussion of the difficulties which it itself engenders. Trust and a number of other relationships cannot be commanded or decreed, they grow or are won. As pointed out earlier (III(8 b)), if two people face a difficulty together, mutual trust or confidence may be generated; if one man gives another a small task which he can overcome but which extends him confidence may grow.

V So far all in the groups considered have been regarded as starting together in the same state of ignorance of the system described. As time goes on this will become a less reasonable assumption in any organization. Quite apart from this the impact on men varies with age and experience as well as personality. Broad levels of age and experience may be distinguished as requiring differences of emphasis in the presentation of the system.

1 In middle management, where men are being promoted to positions of responsibility for the work and progress of others as well as their own, what is valuable is that they should be brought to reconsider their methods of work and review the principles underlying them; to learn about the differences which exist between themselves and their fellows and to see how men of different skills, capacities and personalities can help each other to work together as a team with a common aim.

2 In the top levels of management the issue is quite different. Men have wide experience, often they have their own ways of doing things; and it is often these ways which have brought them to the top and often they are not going to be taught anything new. It is possible, however, that given the opportunity they may come to see what they already know in a fresh light. What is needed here is that they should understand the principles of the training which is being offered to their juniors and by common experience achieve a common understanding of a method of approach. If this is done then they will find it easier to bring the lessons of experience to bear on current issues in such a way as to be valuable to their juniors.

3 For junior men there is an opportunity of being introduced to a systematic approach to getting things done, a system which will help them to ensure thoroughness in themselves and, by establishing a body of common experience in action with others, communication within an organization should be made the easier.

VI Many practical issues arise connected with introducing, developing and maintaining the system set out above within any organization. There is the question where to begin, whether at the top levels, in the middle levels or with newcomers. The advantage of beginning at the top is that those directing the organization can appreciate what is being offered, and are in a position to support and encourage the adoption of the methods throughout the organization. The risk of this is that the training and underlying ideas may themselves come to be considered, within the organization, as 'orthodox' and desirable because favoured by top management. Beginning with beginners has an attraction on the grounds that fewer people would be required to change methods, each could learn the method on joining the organization and in the long run it will permeate the whole. This is, however, a long-term policy and may mean difficulties of older men not understanding younger men for a number of years. The balance of advantage seems to be with beginning not at the top but somewhere near it. The men first trained will often be of great influence in an organization, and be in a position to discuss matters with (and be seen in action by) the top management, who need not yet be committed and may need to be convinced by examples. The effects further afield in the organization should be that the system is accepted because it works, not because the Chairman has decided to back it. Thus the spread should be by voluntary acceptance not by pressures tending to produce conformity.

Appendix 2

Open and closed systems

The following notes by B.B.S. set out in more detail points on this topic.

'There are advantages in having some sort of diagram to illustrate these ideas.

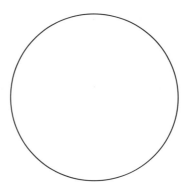

Figure A2.1

1 With a closed system there is a continuous finite boundary (see Figure A2.1). The region within that boundary and its contents can in principle be specified. In the simplest case the boundary is impermeable, our concern is only with any changes or interactions taking place within the boundary. Their consequences also remain within the boundary. In this case the nature of the environment does not matter.

2 With an open system there is still a boundary which delimits the system but either (a) the boundary is permeable or (b) there are gaps or channels which allow communication between the interior and the exterior (see Figure A2.2). Typically a (living) organism draws on its environment for sustenance and rejects or ejects what is not required. It has become customary to use the

picture of a closed system for a mechanism and by contrast one
of an open system for an organism. (I should have thought that a
clock which needs winding to continue to work or a motor car
which needs petrol, oil etc. were better seen as open systems
than as closed – they can continue functioning if supplies of
power or fuel are made available, what they lack is being able to
renew themselves or develop as a young animal does.)

3 Organisms can be seen as open systems in that they can maintain their existence and functioning (given suitable environments). As Lawrence and Lorsch have pointed out (*Developing
Organizations: Diagnosis and Action*, 1969) organizations can, in
addition, change themselves arbitrarily.

4 Typically organisms take in food, digest it, use some and reject
the rest. With human organizations we need something more
complicated:

(a) We may be concerned with the membership of an organization. The model must deal with the intake of members,
their interactions as members and their disassociation from
the organization.

(b) We may be concerned with concepts and ideas. Some are
drawn into the region of an organization and interact with
what was already there. Some and some by-products will be
rejected as obsolete or useless.

(c) One might be concerned with the flow of fees and expenses.
In any real case all three and probably others will be dis-

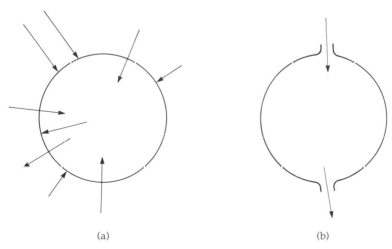

(a)   (b)

Figure A2.2

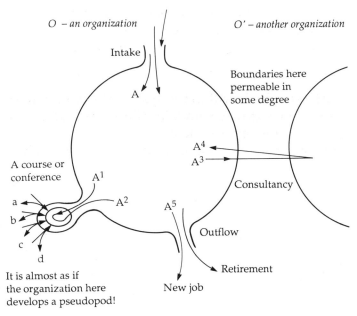

Figure A2.3

cernible – this does not mean that one will need to make one diagram to represent them all. This situation has a parallel with living organisms where one can consider (separately up to a point) the alimentary system, respiratory system, nervous system, and so on.

5 What strikes me as most useful to attempt at this stage is to produce diagrams for 4(a), how the joining of members, their development and eventual disassociation proceed (see Figure A2.3). To attempt to do all this in one diagram is to court confusion. Figure A2.3 is a very rough schematic picture of an organization O with an intake of individuals e.g. A, who after various interactions within O takes part in a 'course' as A^1 and returns as A^2, later having become A^3 visits another organization as a consultant and returns as A^4, and later still leaves O as A^5 for a new job. This is designed to represent in the simplest terms an individual who develops and becomes more experienced and more useful in interacting with other individuals external to the organization (and within). Such interactions benefit the system O:

(a) By means of the information and experience brought back into the system.

(b) By the benefits of the interactions outside being seen to be useful and becoming better known.

(c) by 'sustenance' (e.g. fees) accruing to the system.

6 What are chiefly implied by this open system approach are:

(a) That individuals within the system change progressively by interaction with each other (not illustrated) and with individuals from the environment.

(b) That the change can be organized to be progressive, that the transit of individuals from the system to the environment (by transfer, retirement or other form of release) can be envisaged and to some extent organized, and that the outflow needs to be balanced by an orderly intake and training of the incoming individuals.

(c) What is not illustrated and needs more attention is the interaction between individuals within O which changes A to A^1, A^2 to A^3, A^4 to A^5. This is where there is much scope for improvement.'

Appendix 3

Terminology

It has been said that there are no synonyms in English. In the field this book covers it is clear that there are a number of terms in common use, some with fine differences of meaning. However, many are used very loosely, often as if they were, in fact, synonyms. While there is no way of ensuring that words are always used with precise meanings and it is invariably necessary to listen for how someone else uses a particular term, there are some advantages in using terms consistently. The following are B.B.S.'s views and proposals for reasonable and coherent usage of some key terms, keeping if possible very close to dictionaries.

Strategy, tactics, policy and operations

These are all in the area of planning, of making arrangements concerning the future. Basically *strategy* is concerned with the management of an army. It has come to mean a plan for the achievement of an end or goal usually over a considerable period of time and involving the management of considerable resources; more loosely it is used for a *long-term* or *deep-laid* plan.

Tactics concern the *small-scale activities* which will arise during the conduct of any operation. In the military sense an operation concerns the movement of troops etc. involving engagements with the enemy, in the pursuance of strategy or tactics. In the civil sense it has come to have the same meaning, *mutatis mutandis*.

A *policy* is a *rule* or *set of rules* to guide action when choice arises; it may be especially useful when unexpected situations occur.

Thus in the course of carrying out a strategy circumstances can arise where a small-scale operation is required to achieve some intermediate stage, or to recover time lost. Fresh tactics may well be needed to cope with fresh situations. They will be influenced both by policy and strategy.

Strategy and policy are in some ways independent. The devising of a strategy *could* be carried out without reference to policy. If, however, for some reason events entailed a departure from strategy, then a clear policy could be of great value when choices among different options were needed.

The less clear or less extensive strategy is, the more important it will be to have a policy. Thus we find that people who do not look far ahead (and therefore have no strategy) speak as if policy is all that matters. If aims are obscure or non-existent, all situations as they occur will require consideration. If there is no policy either, all information will need to be balanced and evaluated then and there and it is difficult to see any basis on which choice can be made. Thus the existence of a policy reduces the difficulty of choice. Even where, as has been said, 'I like meeting the buffets of fortune' it is difficult to see how action can be taken or choice made without policy. In such cases policy can be a *substitute* for strategy – this does not mean that the two are interchangeable.

Purpose, aim and related terms

Purpose may be shallow, fleeting, superficial or deep, underlying, firm, profound or unshakeable. In some ways it is useful to think of purpose as a force. A force has direction and when applied does work. Another useful way of thinking of purpose is to link it with 'way' – in the sense it is used when it is said that a boat is 'under way' or 'has way on'. A boat 'under way' is going somewhere, and can be guided and directed; it can also overcome resistance. Without 'way on' progress in a chosen direction cannot be ensured. When looked at thus, purpose can be regarded as a form of energy, somewhat like gravity, and not as it is often used in the sense of a long-term or ultimate aim. Aims arise when purpose is directed and harnessed.

The term *aim* specifies a direction, chosen or preferred, also it is sometimes used for that which is aimed at. Progress is in a, or the, chosen direction.

Goal, target, objective and *end* can each be used for:

1 That which is aimed at or sought.
2 Something to be achieved.
3 An aspiration to be realized.

All can be things, places or states and in principle can be reached or achieved. They can be specified as to nature, position in space or time. It is also often useful to consider their cost.

A *criterion* is a guideline or mark by which to judge success in performance when a job is finished (or at specified stages in its progress).

A *specification* or *standard* is a guide to performance or requirements in material, manpower, or execution for use in planning or while a job is in progress.

An *indicator* is a pointer to or evidence of something. When an indicator becomes established as evidence it can come to be used as a criterion.

There are other terms in common use which are in some way related. These include:

(a) Intent
(b) Intention
(c) Inclination
(d) Interest
(e) Ambition
(f) Aspiration
(g) Preference
(h) Choice
(i) Wish

The foregoing notes on purpose etc. were written from the point of view of one who accepts freewill and holds that when choice arises the outcome is not foreordained. This means that in advance of choice being made, the course of events is not certain or settled, but this in no way precludes the possibility of producing an *account* after the event in terms of cause and effect. (It is important to recognize that only in a trivial sense is such an account an explanation of the course of events.)

There are many people, however, who do not accept this position. For determinists, as they are usually called, it is in principle possible to determine causal influences in advance and so predict what will come about. Where this occurs, as in many inanimate events, the outcome is regarded as having been explained.

It is useful to contrast approaches based on cause and effect leading to explanation with approaches which emphasize purpose and choice raising questions of meaning.

The relevance of this brief outline is that in both approaches terms such as purpose, choice, intention, aim are liable to be used but the implications of the terms may be entirely different. This seems to be very marked in relation to purpose and aim. For a determinist the former seems to mean little more than the direction in which things are going, and it is hard to see that aim can mean anything else.

Terms used in relation to information and its processing

Raw data – when apprehended by some human being raw data must be or must have been processed in some way and can then serve as information.

Observation in the abstract is an application of the special senses.

Observations are the fruits of such application, one important form of information.

Opinions, rumours, reports and *hearsay*, arise from the processing of information. Information when processed can yield:

(a) *Maxims* – rules or principles of conduct usually compactly expressed.
(b) *Principles* – statements which allow no exception.
(c) *Practices* – regular ways of behaving.
(d) *Methods* – ways of doing things.
(e) *Rules of thumb* – generalizations about action which are useful.
(f) *Sayings* – some truths held to be based on man's cumulative experience.
(g) *Saws* – much the same as sayings, possibly sententious.
(h) *Proverbs* – sayings embodied often in alliterative or metaphorical form.
(i) *Precepts* – direction, instruction or rule for conduct, especially moral.
(j) *Advice* – suggestion for conduct.

Some other terms commonly used in the consultancy and training field

Model – a copy of some original or other in specifiable respects e.g. colour, shape, weight etc. The term often carries an implication of reduced scale of size.

Module – sometimes used as a set or body of instructions designed for a particular purpose which can be added to or removed from a larger set without disruption. This sense of the word module receives no support from the *Oxford English Dictionary* where the meaning is given as 'a standard of measurement'. Le Corbusier proposed that man should be the module for architecture.

Thus, if in courses 'exercises' or 'topics' were all taken in sessions of, say, 1 hour and 10 minutes, then '1 hour and 10 minutes' could be called a module for designing training or courses. Working in terms of such a module might have considerable convenience. It is not too difficult to see how if this were done and different topics were taken in different periods the name would come to be used for a block of procedure in a field which is defined.

Consultant – in medical practice the term consultant meant one who is called in by your own doctor. It is unlikely that he would be called in unless he had expertise in the matter which was under consideration. The term defined relation to your own doctor but did not define status. When the National Health Service started a new term was needed to define a certain status and wisely or unwisely the term consultant was used. Since then the use of the term has spread wider to mean someone who is prepared to give advice in return for fees. One would like the term to mean one whose opinion and advice is founded on experience, knowledge and expertise.

Definitions of some other useful concepts

The principle of indirection

When instructions or directions are designed for achieving an objective, the more specific they are the more likely it is that what they do not cover will turn out to be important. Thus the more precisely the syllabus for an examination is defined the more important other aspects of the subject will be found to be; the more precisely the route for a journey is set out the more important becomes the state of the road and the hazards of traffic. (See some examples in Chapters 7 and 21.)

The span of analogy

B.B.S. has found this concept valuable when trying to introduce fresh ideas. One who does not understand a principle at first hearing may do so if it is restated in terms of some different activity. Thus to facilitate some suggestion about, say, giving due notice of a course of action a simple example is the indication of a turn to right or left when driving a car (where the importance of doing so in good time is well-known to anyone who drives and can be readily imagined by most people who do not). It can be helpful to know something of the way of life, tastes or interests of the one who is having difficulty in understanding a principle in order that an example can be given in a field with which he or she is familiar. It is noticeable that people differ in their ability to see principles, some may be said to have a wider span of analogy than others.

Figure and ground

This is a distinction of importance in all perception, referring not so much to the percipient's surroundings but to the attitude of the percipient. If I say I am looking at that picture, the picture is for me the figure; the frame and the walls of the room etc. contribute to the ground. The figure tends to be more clearly seen, with more detail distinguishable. The same may be said of experiences in other sensory fields. The care taken over the surroundings of a picture or the circumstances of a musical performance or of a meal(!) show that we do not only see the picture or hear only the notes in the sonata or only taste the dishes in the meal. Experience is wider, but nevertheless it can be useful to distinguish the figure from the ground.

The principle of means over ends

This principle draws attention to the tendency of what may initially be seen as means for the attainment of some end or other to become ends in themselves. Thus a team which is set up as a very valuable means for getting a particular project carried out may attempt to maintain itself beyond the end of the project; or a negotiator may take up a stance initially to protect some important interests and then lose sight of those interests in maintaining that stance; or a system or procedure may outlast the ends for which it was instituted.

Bibliography

Babington Smith, B. (1969), 'Purpose and Choice' in Whiteley, D. E. H. and Martin, R. (eds), *Sociology, Theology and Conflict*, Basil Blackwell.

Babington Smith, B. and Farrell, B. A. (eds) (1979), *Training in Small Groups*, Pergamon.

Bennis, Warren G. (1976), *The Unconscious Conspiracy: Why Leaders Can't Lead*, AMACOM.

Boulding, Kenneth E. (1956), 'General Systems Theory – The Skeleton of Science', *Management Science*, (April), vol. 2, no. 3.

Burns, T. and Stalker, G. M. (1961), *The Management of Innovation*, Tavistock.

Carroll, Lewis (1876), *The Hunting of the Snark*, Macmillan.

Checkland, Peter (1981), *Systems Thinking, Systems Practice*, John Wiley and Sons.

Checkland, Peter (1986), 'Vickers' Concept of an Appreciative System: a Systemic Account', *Journal of Applied Systems Analysis*, (April), vol. 13.

Coddington A. (1968), *Theories of the Bargaining Process*, Allen and Unwin.

Eilon, Samuel (1981), 'Paradigms, Gestalts and the Obfuscation Factor in Organization Theory', *Omega*, vol. 9, no. 3.

Emery, F. E. and Trist, E. L. (1965), 'The Causal Texture of Organisational Environments', *Human Relations*, vol. 18.

Fisher, Roger and Ury, William (1981), *Getting to Yes*, Houghton Mifflin.

Fisher, Roger with Ury, William (1978), *International Mediation: a Working Guide* (draft edition), Harvard Negotiation Project Publication.

Harvey-Jones, Sir John (1988), *Making It Happen – Reflections on Leadership*, Collins.

Hedberg, Bo L. T., Nystrom, Paul C. and Starbuck, William H. (1976), 'Camping on Seesaws: Prescriptions for a Self-Designing Organization', *Administrative Science Quarterly*, (March), vol. 21.

Hunt, Pearson (1963), *The Case for the Case Study Method*, Cambridge Review.

Kepner, C. H. and Tregoe, B. B. (1965), *The Rotational Manager*, McGraw-Hill.

Kolb, D. A., Rubin, I. M. and McIntyre, J. M. (1974), *Organisational Psychology: An Experiential Approach*, Prentice-Hall.

Janis, Irving L. (1972), *Victims of Groupthink*, Houghton Mifflin.

Lawrence, Paul R. and Lorsch, Jay W. (1969), *Developing Organizations: Diagnosis and Action*, Addison-Wesley.

McGuffie, Duncan (1942), *Spring Onions – The Autobigraphy of Duncan McGuffie*, Faber and Faber.

Metcalfe, J. L. (1974), 'Systems Models, Economic Models and the Causal Texture of Organizational Environments: an Approach to Macro-Organization Theory', *Human Relations*, vol. 27, no. 7.

Metcalfe, J. L. (1974), 'Organisational Strategies and Interorganisational Structure: a Development of the Organisation Set', paper based on study of the behaviour and effectives of Economic Development Committees, London Graduate School of Business Studies.

Raiffa, Howard (1982), *'The Art and Science of Negotiation*, Harvard University Press.

Revans, R. W. (1979), 'The Nature of Action Learning', *Management Education and Development*, (Spring), vol. 10, part 1.

Siegel, S. and Fouraker, L. (1960), *Bargaining and Group Decision Making*, McGraw Hill.

Smallwood, A. J. (1976), 'The Basic Philosophy of Coverdale Training', *Industrial and Commercial Training*, vol. 8, no. 1.

Strauss, Anselm (1978), *Negotiations: Varieties, Contexts, Processes and Social Order*, Jossey-Bass.

Vickers, Sir Geoffrey (1977), 'The Future of Culture' in Linstone, Harold A. and Simmonds, W. H. Clive, *Futures Research – New Directions*, Addison-Wesley.

Woolley, Sir Leonard (1954), *Dead Towns and Living Men*, Lutterworth Press.

Name Index

Adler, Alfred, 43ff
Ashby, W. Ross, 104

Bennis, Warren, 80, 81
Bertalanffy, L. Von, 103
Binet, Alfred, 34
Boulding, Kenneth, 103, 104, 106, 107
Burns, T., 103, 104

Carroll, Lewis, 98
Central Interpretation Unit of Royal Air Force, 5
Checkland, P. B., 109, 110
Coddington, A., 83
Cooper, Andrew, 82
Coverdale, Ralph, vii, ix, 1, 3, 5, 6, 8, 10, 11, 13, 14, 15, 18, 21, 22, 25, 27, 30, 31, 32, 47, 49, 51, 52, 53, 54, 55, 58, 72, 80, 92, 103, 104, 106, 110, 116, 121, 124, 132, 135
Coverdale Organisation, The, vii, ix, 1, 2, 3, 30, 52, 67, 81, 117
Cross, J. G., 83

Delin, P., 18
Dewey, John, 27

Eilon, Samuel, 121
Einstein, Albert, viii
Emery, F. E., 107, 120
Esso Petroleum Company, 10
Experimental Psychology Society, 18

Farrell, B. A., 3
Fisher, Roger, 74, 82, 86, 90, 93
Fouraker, L., 83
Freud, Sigmund, 43ff

Harvard Business School, 27
Harvard Negotiation Project, 74, 89
Harvey-Jones, Sir John, 1
Hedberg, Bo L. T., 114, 120
Heisenberg, Werner Karl, 131
Hunt, Pearson, 27

Janis, Irving L., 101
Jung, Carl Gustav, 43ff

Kennedy, President J. F., 101
Kepner, C. H., 25
Kolb, D., 26, 109

Lawrence, Paul R., 147
Le Corbusier, Charles-Édouard Jeanneret, 154
Linstone, Harold A., 122
Lorsch, Jay W., 147

McGuffie, Duncan, 121
Martin, R., 43
Metcalfe, 107, 120
Miles, Matthew, 52

National Health Service, 154
Nielsen's A. C., 5

O'Sullivan, 89

Raiffa, Howard, 88, 89
Revans, R. W., 30, 31
Roche, Seamus, 15, 135

Siegel, S., 83
Simmonds, W. H. Clive, 122
Smallwood, Alex, 82, 84, 87
Stalker, G. M., 103, 104
Steel Company of Wales, 5, 10, 52
Strauss, Anselm, 87

Training Services Agency, 119
Tregoe, B. B., 25
Trist, E. L., 107, 120

United Nations Development
    Programme, 74
Ury, William, 74

Vickers, Sir Geoffrey, 109, 110,
    111, 122
Voltaire, 88

Wellens, John, 89
Whitegate Refinery of Irish
    Refining Company, 15
Whiteley, D. E. H., 43
Woolley, Sir Leonard, 84

Subject Index

Action:
  bringing release of tension, 10
  essential for function of
    managers, 10, 15, 80, 136
  important in developing
    judgement, 27
  important in group formation
    and development, 8ff, 24, 25,
    138
Action learning, 30ff
Agents in negotiations, 72, 74, 84,
    85
Aims, vii, 17, 20, 22, 24, 25, 31,
    42, 48ff, 61, 63, 64, 65, 72, 87,
    88, 90, 94, 99, 100, 115, 118,
    125, 131, 137, 142
  common comprehension of, 15,
    80, 138, 139
  different aspects of, 48ff
  different words used to
    describe, 48ff, 151
  meaning of term to a
    determinist, 42, 152
  procedure for establishing by
    asking 'why?', 46ff
  tiers or hierarchies of, 49ff, 64
Aims of Coverdale work, 79ff, 94
Analogy, use of, 155
Analysis and synthesis, 15
Assessment of performance and
    talents, 55ff
Assumptions, 78, 86, 87, 97, 101
Authority:
  flow in hierarchical structure,
    72, 140ff

one theme of Coverdale
    Training, 24

Balance:
  between task and process, 51ff,
    139
  Hedberg's aphorisms as balance
    between extremes, 199
  need for awareness to maintain
    balance between task and
    process, 53
  of attention needed between
    successes and difficulties,
    58ff, 101ff
Bargaining, 83ff
  situations not conformable to
    team-building, 84
Bay of Pigs invasion, 101
Binet test, 34ff
Boards of directors, see Directors

Case study method, 27
  contrasted with Coverdale
    Training, 27ff
Change (in organizations), 119ff,
    136ff
Chart, four-column, 38, 40
Choice, 49, 151
  ethical considerations and, 125
  not same as decision, 22
  purpose and choice, 42ff, 122
'Choice to help', 4, 31, 47, 61, 65,
    75, 78, 84, 86, 87, 89, 91, 93,
    96, 128
  how far to extend, 128ff

Climate (in organizations), 119
Closed (and open)
    problems/situations, *see* Open
    and closed
    problems/situations
Cognitive learning, 26
Collective responsibility, 85
Commitment:
    of recipient one factor affecting
    communication of
    instructions, 62
    to implement plans increases
    with scope to contribute to
    them, 64
Communication:
    between an organization and its
    environment, 108
    between steerers and joiners,
    63ff
    channels in an organization,
    115
    information and instructions
    between leaders and
    followers of, 68ff
    within a hierarchical structure,
    125, 141ff
Company philosophy, statements
    of, 126
Consultants, 82, 119ff
    meaning, 154
Cosy groups, 99, 101
Courage, 80, 139
Coverdale groups and teams, 4,
    84, 86, 87, 112
Coverdale Training, vii, ix, 1ff,
    13ff, 18, 21, 27, 31, 36, 38,
    51ff, 57, 60, 67, 68, 74, 76, 79,
    86, 92ff, 98, 103, 107, 113,
    114, 131, 132
    aims of Coverdale work, 79ff,
    94
    consultancy and OD work, 79ff,
    81, 119
    early courses and lessons, 8ff
    emphasis on aims (as opposed
    to 'here and now'), 130ff

origins, 5
Part 2 course, 54, 55, 60, 67, 80,
    81, 82, 95, 113, 114
principles, 3, 84, 87
systems thinking and, 103ff
themes, 24
Crisis management, 46, 114, 115
Criteria of success, *see* Success
    criteria
Criterion, meaning, 152
Cultural goals and values, 108
Culture, 122, 127, 128

Decisions, decision making and
    decision theory, 22ff
Delegation, 72ff
    content of briefing and, 72ff
    definition, 71
    development of subordinates
    and, 72ff
Demonstrations in Coverdale
    Training, 10ff, 33
Depth psychology, 5
Determinists, 43, 152
    meaning of terms, purpose etc.
    to determinists, 42, 153
Development:
    groups of, 4, 54, 92ff
    individuals of, 4, 92ff
    organizations of, *see*
    Organization development
    small firms of, 121ff
    subordinates of, 63, 72, 73
    teams of, *see* Team formation
    and development
Directors (and boards of
    directors), 124ff
    choice and, 125, 128ff
    courses for directors, 79, 124,
    128, 133
Disadvantages and errors in
    systems of training, 3ff
Discovery:
    learning and, 8
    not enough, 14

Economic Development
  Committees, 108
Emotions and feelings in
  structured and structureless
  situations, 10
Enthusiasm:
  not enough, ix, 14
  teambuilding and, 99
Entropy, 107
Environmental influences on
  organizations, 114, 120
Environmental responsiveness
  and environmental
  effectiveness (distinguished
  by Metcalfe), 108, 120
Environments:
  interaction with, 81
  richly joined, 108
  study of and effects on
  organizations, 107ff
Ethical issues and considerations,
  81, 89, 121, 122
Ethical systems, 103
Ethics and choice prime concerns
  for people at top levels of
  organizations, 125
Experience not enough alone to
  produce learning, 13ff
Experiential method, 13
Exploratory approach, 13ff

'Figure-ground', 44
  meaning of concept, 155
Followers, functions of, 68ff
Free will, 48ff
Freudian:
  approach, 5
  -based interpretations, 5
  theory, 5, 34

General method:
  necessary for tackling
  difficulties and getting things
  done, 14
Geneva arms reduction talks, 88

'Getting to know' others:
  how this happens, 74ff, 90ff
  importance, 74ff, 85, 86, 90, 139
'Getting to Yes', 74ff, 82ff, 90
Goal, target, objective, end:
  meaning, 43, 151
Group dynamics vii, *see also*
  T-Groups
Group formation and
  development, 4, 8, 54, 92ff
'Group Project' in early Coverdale
  courses, 8
Groups:
  'open' systems as, 101
  power of, 95, 96
  reasons for working in groups,
  137
  teams and organizations
  compared, 118ff
  vehicles to enable individuals to
  learn as, 92

'Hawthorne effect', 98
Heisenberg Principle of
  Uncertainty, 131
'Help or hinder', 55ff
Honesty, 31, 80
Human interaction, 51ff, 86ff

Imitation learning, 26
Incidents, treatment in Coverdale
  practice, 38ff
Indicator, meaning, 152
Indicators of progress, 49
Indirection, Principle of, 28, 95
Individual and team
  development, 93ff
Induction of newcomers into
  organizations, 115
Inductive method/learning, 13,
  31, 131
Inductive thinking, 135
Information:
  communication of information
  between leaders and
  followers, 68ff

need to adapt to recipients'
level of skill, 11
processing, 81, 153ff
terms used in relation to
information and its
processing, 153ff
Insight (or 'discovery'), 8, 28
Instructions, communication of,
68ff
Interaction:
between groups or
departments, 81
with the environment, 81
see also Human interaction
Interpretation, based on shared
experience rather than
theory, 34

Jelling (of a group), 8, 80
Joiners, duties and responsibilities
of, 65ff
Joining, *see* Steering and joining
Judgement, development of, 27ff

Leaders and followers, 67ff
Leadership and Coverdale
programmes, 67ff
Leading and following, 60
Learning:
by doing, 26, 30ff
styles and a systematic
approach, 27ff
system (cyclic), 27ff
talk of learning by experience
misleading, 15
to learn not enough, 14
two distinct theories, 57ff
what matters is to get things
done, 27
Lectures in Coverdale Training, 8,
10
Listening, 64, 65, *see also* Support
Listening and support, one theme
of Coverdale Training, 24
Loyalties, 5, 80, 82ff, 85, 86, 91,
125

Management, different aspects of
management, 53
Management training:
approach to get managers to
take responsibility to manage
people, ix
different training needs of
senior managers and
directors, 80ff, 124
need and warrant for
management training, 5, 6ff,
136
principles of training
applicable, 6ff
three stages, 7ff, 126ff, 144
Maxims, meaning, 153
Mechanistic systems, 103
Mediation, 86
Model(s), 106
getting to know people of, 75
meaning, 153
Module, meaning, 154
Morale, 58
Multiple choice tests, effect on
education, 14, 18

Negotiation, 72, 74ff, 82ff, 86ff,
90ff, 92, 94
community of aims and, 87ff
comparison of work at Harvard
with Coverdale training, 74ff
definition, 85
expected behaviour and, 88ff

Objective(s), vii, 17, 42ff
bargaining process of, 83
Obligation (mutual) between an
organization and those
joining, 6, 135, 141
Observation, 16, 24, 33ff, 50, 54ff,
64, 65, 75, 81, 100, 118, 125,
138ff
development sequence in
respect to observation, 41,
138

importance of including fruits
of observation in review, 15
improving skill, 36ff
meaning, 153
review of action entails, 26
stages in making observations,
32ff, 55, 100
Observational systems, 36ff
Observer(s), value of being, 13,
32ff
'Obstenacity', 58
Open approach, 8
Open and closed
problems/situations, 10, 14ff,
18ff, 49, 54, 98
systems, 146ff
Open situations:
improving group performance
best regarded as open
situation, 101
value of teamwork when
tackling, 98
Open system approach, 149
Opening up and closing down,
19ff, 25, 49, 98
Organic systems, 103
Organisms and open systems,
146ff
Organization climate/culture, 127
Organization development (OD),
81, 107, 118ff, 126
compared with development of
teams, 186ff
Organization theories, 121
Organizations:
difference between setting up
an organization and
maintaining or modifying it,
113
distinguished from groups,
112ff, 124
environmental influences and,
114
open systems as, 123, 124, 128,
147ff

organizing and, 112ff
systematic approach and, 116ff
value of three-stage system of
training in maintaining
durability of organizations, 7,
126ff
Outlook, differences between
individuals, 17, 44ff, 138
Outward bound type exercises, 68

Perceptual demonstrations, 10
Performance assessment, 54ff
Philosophy (company), 126
Planning:
definition of a plan, 136, 142
different meanings, 17, 45ff
process, *see* Process planning
two ways of planning, 11ff
Policy, meaning, 150ff
Power, 44, 88
Powers and credentials, 89
Practice, meaning, 153
Practice necessary to apply
knowledge, 14
Practice of Management
Principles course, 92
Practice of Teamwork course, 92
Precepts, meaning, 153
Principle(s):
Coverdale Training of, 3, 84, 87
'do as you would be done by'
of, 85
'fairness' of, 85
meaning, 153
practices and, 7, 28ff
proceedings and transactions
of, 84ff
rules of thumb and, 13, 28ff
steering and joining of, 62ff
that commitment relates to
scope to contribute, 69
that enthusiasm is not enough,
14
that experience, realization or
discovery not enough, 14

that information needs to relate to level of skill of recipient, 11ff

that it is important for an individual to realize potential, 28

that there are two ways of planning, 11ff

training (general) of, 6ff

two ways of planning of, 19ff

Principle of indirection, 28

definition, 154

Principle of means over ends, definition, 154

Principle of Uncertainty (Heisenberg), 131

Problem setting, 15

Problem solving, 10

'a systematic approach' and, 24ff

limitations, 20

Problems and solutions, risks of thinking in these terms, 14

Procedural matters, should take priority in reviewing group performance, 86, 101

Proceedings, 5

definition, 79ff, 125

Proceedings and transactions, 79ff, 125

summary of key points, 90ff

Process:

interaction, 52, 86, 139

issues in hierarchical groups, 143ff

sub-divided into means, methods, human interaction, 52, 86, 139

task, and, *see* Task and process

Process planning, 24, 98, 112, 113ff, 118

Process skills, 52, 54ff, 80, 94

Proverbs, meaning, 153

Purpose:

form of energy, as, 22, 24, 151ff

meaning of purpose, aim and related terms, 151ff

meaning to determinist, 42, 152

meaning to those accepting free will, 42, 152

Purpose (and choice), 16, 42ff, 122

Reciprocating engine theories of decision making, 22

contrasted with turbine theory of action, 22ff

Responsibility (personal), 51, 54, 65, 72, 80

Review:

content needs to change between one level and another in an organization, 116ff

distinct aspects (procedural issues; personal skills/interpersonal relations), 40, 101

importance of including fruits of review in further work, 15

plan to improve and, 100ff, 125

Risk, 49

Ritual, 28ff

Role playing, 80

Rules of thumb, 13, 28ff

meaning, 153

Scientific method, 15

Self-designing organizations, 114

Self-organizing organizations, 120

Self-regulating group, 112, 113

Self-regulating organization, 7

Sensitivity training, 119

Skills, as one theme of Coverdale Training, 24

Skills exercise, 55, 58

Small group methods, 52, 96, 118

Span of analogy, 155

Specification, standard, meaning, 152

Static systems, 103

Steering and joining, 38ff, 60ff, 67, 71, 94, 97, 113, 114
  principles, 62ff
Strategy, meaning, 150ff
Structure:
  group, 140
  hierarchical, 140ff
  organizational, 125
Success, doctrine of, 57ff
  effects of emphasis on success, 58
Success criteria, 25, 49, 100, 141
Support, 25, 64, 80, *see also* Listening and support
Synthesis and analysis, 15
Systematic approach:
  action learning and, 30ff
  complete system as, 16
  development, 13ff
  general method, programme of learning from experience as, 16, 26
  learning styles and, 26ff
  logic and, 16
  model of organization as, 116ff, 141ff
  negotiation and, 131
  one 'theme' of Coverdale Training as, 24
  possible developments, 130ff
  problem solving and, 24ff
  systems thinking and, 103
  whether appropriate for senior managers and directors, 131ff
  whether appropriate in all situations, 131
'Systematic Approach to Getting Things Done' (June 1965 paper), 135ff
Systems:
  meaning, 103
  Boulding's classification, 104ff
  Coverdale's and Boulding's classifications compared, 106
  general systems theory, 104ff

groups as systems, 79, 101
kinds of systems, R. Coverdale's ideas, 103
open and closed, 104, 146ff
systems thinking and, 103ff
Systems thinking and Coverdale, 109ff
Systems of training:
  how they develop, 4
  reasons for errors creeping in, 3ff

Tactics, meaning, 150ff
Talent assessment, 54ff
Task mesmerization, 52
Task and process, 51ff, 86, 139ff
  distinction as teaching device, 53
Tasks:
  Coverdale Training in, 9ff, 51, 67ff
  different types, 51
  origin of use in Coverdale Training, 9ff
  'trivial', 68
Teaching devices, 3
Team formation and development, 54, 60, 75, 82, 84, 93ff, 97ff, 139ff
  means of lessening anxiety as, 98
Teamwork, 9, 31, 53, 64, 75, 80, 92ff, 94, 96, 97ff
  Coverdale Training and, 92ff
  not original aim of Coverdale Training, 94
  open situations and, 98
  poor ultimate aim, 95
  relationship with level of performance, 99ff
Terminology, 150ff
T-Group situation in early Coverdale courses, 8
T-Groups, 5, 99, 119
Themes of Coverdale Training, 24

Thought, a framework for action, 15

Training:
  collecting and transmitting information need for all in, 70
  different training needed at different levels, 144ff
  principles, 6ff
  where too start, 144ff *see also* Management training

Transactions, 93, 97, 123
  definition, 79, 84
  effect of differences of individual outlook on transactions, 46
  principles, 84ff

Transactions and proceedings, 79ff, 125
  summary of key points, 90ff

True–false choice tests, effect on education, 14, 18

Trust, 77, 84, 85, 140
  hierarchical situations in, 143ff

Turbine theory of action, 21ff, 25, 43, 49, 101

Values, 28, 133

Ways of talking (WOTs) 3

Why?, different meanings, 46ff

Working accommodations, 78, 80

Working parties, 60ff